D1569510

Overcoming Life's Obstacles

Library of Congress Control # 1-901473881

ISBN – 13:978-0615782522

ISBN – 10:0615782523

Connect with Stephanie Lahart

http://about.me/stephanie.lahart

https://twitter.com/1lahart

https://www.facebook.com/1lahartstephanie

http://1lahartstephanie.blogspot.com/

http://stephanielahart1.wordpress.com/

Feel free to connect with me on Google+ as well.

Special Thanks

First and foremost, I would like to give honor and thanks to God for using me to write a book that is so powerful that it will impact and change people's lives. There's no way I would've been able to write *Overcoming Life's Obstacles* without your guidance. Thank you for the strength and courage to write my first book.

I would also like to thank my beautiful daughter! I know deep down in my heart that I couldn't have written this book without your love, support, and help. Thank you SO very much for taking the time to read through every passage that I wrote and giving me your honest opinion. Thank you for your patience and understanding while I wrote my book. You are truly my inspiration and God couldn't have blessed me with a better child. You're quite a young lady and I respect you. You're also an amazing person and you have a beautiful spirit. You are my heartbeat and I love you with all of my heart and soul.

Table of Contents

INTRODUCTION

I ask that you please read this book with an open mind. Some of my passages may touch a nerve, but I challenge you to open yourself up to becoming a better YOU. Personal-Growth is a good thing, but as we all know, sometimes facing the truth can be difficult at first. I encourage you to embrace every emotion that you may feel. I wrote each passage with a different purpose. I wanted to write a book that was different from any other book on the market.

While reading *Overcoming Life's Obstacles,* you can expect all of my passages to be captivating. I don't sugar-coat anything. My sole purpose for writing this book was to impact and change lives. I believe that my job as an author is to write without limits. That's exactly what I did.

Let your journey begin! As you read through each new passage you will gain wisdom, insight, and feel an overall sense of empowerment. This book will also provide awareness, lots of food-for-thought, encouragement, and inspiration. If you're sincerely ready for change, then you've picked the right book.

Forgiveness

I'm going to be up front and honest with you. It can be very difficult to forgive someone when they've hurt or betrayed you. But, we must remember that forgiving someone is NOT for them, it's for us. Let me explain why.

When we hold things in our hearts that people have done to us, what we're really doing is giving them power over us. Forgiving someone is very beneficial to you. It sets you free and releases you from the hurt and pain that you've been carrying around. It is definitely a release and it frees your mind. Forgiveness is a MUST if you want to move forward in your life. You can't move forward and be free if you're holding on to dead weight. Living with hate in your heart for someone is surely going to consume you, not the person that you're mad or upset with. Choosing to forgive someone is not your way of saying "It's okay what you did to me." Forgiving someone gives you the upper hand. It gives you peace within yourself. You gain control over yourself. They don't gain control over you.

Has anyone ever brought up a person's name that you hadn't forgiven? Do you remember how you reacted or how you felt? Do you realize how much energy goes into being mad at somebody and holding a grudge against someone? I'll say it again: Forgiving someone is not for them, it's for you. You have to get to a point where you really understand this. It's for you!

Look at it this way: When you keep unforgiveness in your heart, it's like poisoning your body. You're polluted with foul STUFF. It's like a garbage can. You're keeping stinky garbage in your system and it's rotten. You need to take it out and get rid of it. When you let go of what's weighing you down, you will feel like a renewed person.

Try it! Allow yourself to be free. Let it go...Let it go...Let it go. It's not worth taking away the happiness from your life. It's just not worth it! Unforgiveness in your heart literally takes away from your life little by little until it overtakes you and controls you. It robs you of who you really are as a person. Trust me, it does.

Encourage Yourself

As humans, when we do something right, we like to hear kind words like: "Great job! Awesome! Way to go! Right on! Wow, I'm so happy for you!" etc.

Ask yourself, who doesn't like to be acknowledged for a job well done? Compliments are great to receive, but we have to ensure that if we don't receive the recognition we feel that we deserve, we don't fall apart, and/or get discouraged.

We have to learn how to encourage ourselves when nobody else does. When you learn to encourage yourself, you stay uplifted in all areas of your life. We can't depend on people to always be there, but we can depend on ourselves. Think about it. Every time you feel yourself getting discouraged, try encouraging yourself and speaking positively. As time passes by, you will learn to rely more on yourself and get through any situation that you may be facing.

There's so much power in encouragement. Encouragement means to boost, lift, praise, support, and inspire someone. Believe in yourself and know what you represent. When you clearly know who you are and what you stand for, inner confidence will guide you through.

There's also another point I would like to make: Everybody will NOT be happy for you. Everybody will

NOT rejoice with you. Everybody will NOT believe in you. Some people want to see you fail. But, failure is not an option for you! Encourage yourself. Tell yourself, "I'm proud of me, and that's all that matters." Encourage yourself, believe in yourself, and love yourself. Never doubt who you are. Be your own personal cheerleader. Self-encouragement is a powerful tool. Don't be afraid to utilize it.

You're going to be OKAY

I know that you may be going through some really tough and trying times right now, but you're going to be okay. I know that you're still dealing with the hurt and the pain from your past, but you're going to be okay. I know that you feel like giving up and throwing in the towel, but, please don't, you're going to be okay. I know that you feel like you just can't take it anymore, but keep on pushing anyways, you're going to be okay. I know that you're tired of being mistreated and misunderstood, but you're going to be okay. I know that you're tired of everybody depending on you when you wish you had somebody to depend on, but, you're going to be okay. I know that you're tired of always having to be the strong one for the family, but you're going to be okay.

I know that you're tired of your kids giving you a hard time, but you'll be okay. I know that you're tired of working long hours and still having to struggle to get by, but, no worries, you're going to be okay. I know that you're tired of all the fussing and fighting, but you're going to be okay. I know that you're tired of feeling lonely and wish that you had somebody to love, but you're going to be okay. I know that you're tired of being sick in your body, but, by God's grace and mercy, you will be healed. You're going to be okay. I know that you're tired of disappointing yourself and others that love and care for you, but it's going to be okay. I know that you're tired of pretending like you have it all together when all hell is breaking loose in your life, but be encouraged, ALL is well.

You're going to be okay because our God is in control. He will give you peace in the midst of a storm. All you have to do is talk to him. There is no right or wrong way to talk to him. Just talk to him like you're talking to a regular person. He knows all and he sees all. He knows our struggles. He knows our pain. He knows our disappointments. He knows, He KNOWS! We can depend on God to see us through. Make no mistake about that. He loves and cares for us. Everything works together for the good of those who love the Lord. Not some things, but ALL things. You're going to be okay!

Disowned

I dedicate this passage to the disowned. I can only imagine your pain. Someone who you thought loved you pushed you away and no longer wants to have anything to do with you.

How could anyone disown you because you got pregnant at an early age? How could anyone disown you because you married somebody of a different race? How could anyone disown you because you didn't go to the school or college that they wanted you to? How could anyone disown you because you came out and told them that you were gay or lesbian? How could anyone disown you because you didn't live up to their expectations? How could anyone disown you because you decided to become a different religion than they are? How could anyone disown you because you decided to get piercing and tattoos on your body? How could anybody disown you because you made a horrible mistake and used drugs?

How could anyone disown you because you didn't take the route that they wanted you to go? How could anyone disown you because you had a biracial child? How could anyone disown you because your best friend is mixed with another race that they're not fond of? How could anyone disown you simply because they can't control you? How could anyone disown you because you decided to tell the truth about all of the bad things that

7

were going on in the family and they didn't want to believe or accept it? How could anyone disown you because you weren't "perfect" in their eyes? How could anyone disown you because you decided to tell the truth? How could anyone disown you because you allowed alcohol to take over your life?

Let's face it! Everybody makes mistakes in their life and they sometimes wish that they could turn back the hands of time, but they can't. If you say that you love somebody, you can't make the choice to disown them because YOU have a problem with what they did. I'm sure that if you took a good look at yourself, you're not "Mr. /Mrs. Perfect" either.

We don't have a right to disown or stop loving somebody just because we don't like what they did or said. It's not that serious. Unconditional love means accepting people for who they are. Showing real love is not by being controlling.

How could any mother or father disown their child? Your children are YOUR seeds. Just what are you saying to your children when you disown them? "I love you, but only if I can control what you are, what you become, what you do, etc." Shame on you! It's wrong and there's nothing you could say that would make it right. How does your own family disown you? Aren't families supposed to stick together? We should be able to call on

8

our families for support and love. Above all, if nobody else accepts us for who were are, our family should.

To the disowned, don't feel guilty for what you did or what you said. You are your own person and you did nothing wrong. Nobody in this world is perfect. Not even the person or people who disowned you. Remember that they are the ones with the problem. I know that it may be very difficult dealing with the fact that you were disowned, but know this: You are somebody! You are somebody VERY special! Don't be ashamed of who you are!

Don't Suppress Your Feelings, Talk About It

Many people go through life believing that the best way to handle what they are feeling is to keep their mouth closed and deal with it inwardly. They tell themselves that they're okay, but on the inside, they feel tormented. When you keep your feelings inside and never talk about them, they will eventually affect other parts of your life. Knowing how to communicate is a very powerful tool and it's essential to our lives. Your feelings are valid and you have a right to talk about them.

Suppressing your emotions and feelings will physically and mentally harm you. It will wear you down and cause you to feel drained all of the time. Anger, bitterness, the feeling of loneliness, low self-esteem, and a number of other feelings will sit there and eat away at you until you do something about it. That's why it's important to get whatever feelings that you're feeling out in the open. Do you realize that a lot of people battle with addictions because they suppress their feelings? Your suppressed emotions will, in most cases, consume you little by little.

Speak up! Talk about it and don't hold it in. Let your voice be heard. If you need help with communicating your feelings, it's okay to seek help. I know a lot of people who have a problem with seeking help from a counselor, but I'm here to tell you, there's nothing wrong with getting the help that you need. There's no shame in reaching out for help. Reaching out for help means that you've realized that you can't do it alone and you need direction. There's NOTHING wrong with asking for help.

Quick example: Let's say that you were never good at math and you never asked for help. Well, that means that you're going to keep getting the answers wrong unless you reach out and ask for help. Once you ask for help and you get an understanding of how to work out the problems, you'll feel relieved. It's the same concept with our feelings. Keep that in mind.

You're Stronger than You Thought

I would like to dedicate this passage to the women, men, girls, and boys who grew up without a mother, father, or neither parent. So many children are being raised by their grandparents or other family members, are in the foster care system, or are growing up on the streets doing what they have to do to survive. You're still here! You're still standing! YOU have a story!

You didn't do anything wrong. You didn't get to choose your life. You were born into this world as an innocent little boy or girl. Growing up may have been difficult and, I'm sure, confusing too, dealing with the fact that somebody didn't love you.

Didn't love you enough to stick around. Didn't love you enough to change their ways. Didn't love you enough to make things right. Didn't love you enough to stop using drugs or alcohol. Didn't love you enough to stay out of jail and prison. Didn't love you enough to get the help that they needed. Didn't love you enough to call you. Didn't love you enough to make it to your special occasions. Didn't love you enough to keep his or her word. Didn't love you enough to come visit you. Didn't love you enough to get off the streets. Didn't love you enough to simply be your Mom or Dad.

Parents have an obligation to their children to raise, mold, and shape them in the way that they should be. Children should be able to trust and believe in the people who created them and gave them life. Parents should love, support, encourage, and be there every step of the way ensuring that their children grow up to be well-rounded adults that are ready for the real world. You didn't get this opportunity and it doesn't seem fair. But guess what? Through it all, you're still here, you're still standing, and YOU have a story!

You made it through in spite of all the obstacles that you faced. You could've given up and thrown in the towel, but you didn't. You could've taken the easy way out, but you didn't. Give yourself credit. You are special in every single way. Don't allow anybody to make you feel any different. You made it! I commend you! I salute you! I give honor to you!

Trying to Fill a Void

Do you do things to try to fill a void in your life?

Some people go shopping to try to fill a void. Some people sleep around trying to fill a void. There are a lot of people who suffer from emotional eating by trying to fill a void. It's never easy to lose a loved one. It can cause some people to act out and do things that they aren't proud of. Many people use drugs and alcohol thinking that it will fill their void. What are some of the things you do to try to fill a void?

That's an important question to ask yourself so that you can acknowledge the problem. Sometimes we don't know what else to do, so we'll do things that'll make us feel good for the moment. All we want to do is make the void go away, not realizing that it's still going to be there until we face it.

Having a void in your life can cause you to feel lonely. When you have a void in your life, you can sometimes feel a sense of emptiness within. There's nothing to feel bad about. You're not alone. Many people live their lives trying to fill some kind of void. The first step to getting better is to admit that you have a void. You have to be honest with yourself before you can move forward. Once you've acknowledged that you have a problem and that you're trying to fill a void, get some help. It's very important to talk about what caused you to have that void. Once you understand what caused the void, then you can move forward and find HEALTHY ways to overcome the empty piece in life that you're missing.

Violated

Isn't it amazing how all of us are born as innocent little children? Babies are beautiful little bundles of joy. As adults, we enjoy watching them grow and learn different things like: learning how to crawl, taking their first steps, holding their bottle for the first time, feeding themselves, and all the other things that bring a big smile to our faces.

As we grow up, things and people help shape and mold us into the people that we become. Sometimes in our lives, we become a victim of something that nobody should ever have to endure or experience.

I'm talking about being violated. Many people have experienced some kind of violation in their lives. It's a subject that nobody likes to discuss because of the shame. Let's get one thing straight! Don't blame yourself for what happened to you. You were taken advantage of by somebody who knew better, and they had no right to do what they did, period!

So many people go through life living with the shame of what happened to them. It's not fair to you that you have to live life with emotional and mental scars. In some severe cases, people have physical scars depending on what took place. People deal with what happened in many ways. Some choose to suppress it and act as if it never happened because they don't want to face the fact that something like that happened to them.

Here are some other things that someone may go through: having a tough time in relationships, serious intimacy issues, lack of trust, little-to-no confidence in their self, resentments, anger issues, emotional damage, self-destructive behavior, etc.

You were robbed of your innocence. Some people are open about what happened, but there are still a large percentage of people who never discuss it. Molestation and rape is absolutely NOT your fault.

You don't have anything to be ashamed of. Remember, YOU were taken advantage of. Don't allow anybody to make you feel like you caused this or that you brought this on yourself. That's pure nonsense!

If you haven't talked about it or dealt with it, please get help. It's not fair that you have to keep this inside of you and not get it out. If you're not a huge fan of counseling, talk to somebody that you can confide in and completely trust.

My prayer is to see you get set free. Free from all of the shame, hurt, and pain. You're not alone. This happens to more people than you think. It's not right, it's WRONG, and it has to stop.

If you have kids, make sure that you talk to them, and if they ever come to you, make sure you listen and believe them. Molestation and rape doesn't just happen with strangers. Many families have ill-minded people that hurt their family members too. Don't be in denial, be aware.

I pray right now in the name of Jesus, that God will heal your every wound and give you peace.

Until You Get Enough

Until YOU get enough of what you're going through, no matter what advice a person gives you, you'll continue to go through the same thing.

Have you ever known somebody that says, "I've had ENOUGH," BUT, days, weeks, or years later, you see them still putting up with the same crap. That's because they didn't really mean it when they said that they've had enough. They spoke it out of their mouth, but their heart was still in it. The truth of the matter is, sometimes the person has to go through the fire themselves in order to really learn a lesson.

There's nothing like getting hurt until you reach a point where it breaks you down. There's nothing like experiencing disappointment, until it's looking you straight in the face. There's nothing like being lied to by somebody you fully trusted, but now you recognize the truth. There's nothing like helping somebody over and over again, just to be burned in the end.

Have you had enough yet? Are you sick and tired of being sick and tired? How much more are you willing to put up with? Is this just a waste of your time? You say that you've had enough of his/her cheating. But as soon as they sweet talk you, you're right back in their arms, totally dismissing what they've done to you. You say you're sick and tired of lending money. But as soon as someone shares their sob story with you, you're at the bank or pulling out your wallet. You say that you're sick and tired of EVERYTHING, but you keep finding yourself pulled back into your misery.

What is it going to take for you to be good to yourself? It's one thing to be kind, but it's another story when you allow people to start taking advantage of you and have you on a roller coaster ride of emotions. You're up one minute, down the next, and being twisted in every direction. It's time to put you first! The next time you say that you've had enough, mean it and stand on your word without wavering.

Are Your Friends REALLY Your Friends

Let's talk about friends. Unfortunately, some people use this word very loosely. You can't call everybody your friend.

A genuine friend is not jealous of you or what you have. A genuine friend supports you and they're there for you to lean on. A genuine friend is honest with you and they're not afraid to tell you when you're wrong. A genuine friend does NOT gossip about you behind your back or share your personal business with anybody else. A genuine friend does NOT judge you. They love you for who you are. A genuine friend is somebody that you can confide in and you know that it stays between you and them. A genuine friend will cry with you. A genuine friend understands. A genuine friend encourages you to go after your dreams and they believe in you. A genuine friend makes time for you. A genuine friend knows how to compromise and allow the other to have their space.

It's important to realize that our friends have other things going on in their lives as well. We should be careful not to feel like we're suffocating them and being selfish wanting them all to ourselves. You have to keep the friendship on a healthy level. A genuine friend has good communication and listening skills. This is very important because a lack of communication in any relationship can cause problems. When you have good communication, there's less room for issues because you've both learned to talk it out. A genuine friend sticks around. They're your friend because they love and care for you, not because of what you have. I want to reiterate, true friends do NOT show any kind of jealousy. No matter how you try to justify it, jealousy has no place in any kind of relationship.

Jealousy is not something that should be taken lightly. If a person is showing you signs of jealousy and they're supposed to be your friend, beware! Jealousy is wicked! It will cause people to do all sorts of things.

So, I'll leave you with this question and I want you to take a good look at your friends. Are your friends really your friends? Be honest with yourselves. If your so-called "friends" don't add to your life, it's time to reevaluate why you're allowing them to take up that space. It's better to have genuine friends who really value your friendship than to have people around you that don't do anything to add to your life.

Body Image

I think that we have all complained about something that we don't like about our bodies. But, by the end of this passage, I hope that you have a different attitude about your body.

Everybody has a unique body of their own. We were not all meant to look alike. We have to learn how to accept and embrace what we were given. It's important to not allow what others feel and say about us influence how we feel about ourselves. Find the beauty in yourself. This goes for men and women.

Women, stop comparing yourself to the next woman. As women, we want larger breasts, tighter buns, sexier legs, fuller lips, flatter stomachs, less wrinkles, and everything else under the sun. Stop it! You have to love yourself from the inside out. That's what's most important.

Your appearance on the outside will NOT change how and what you feel about yourself overall. You think that getting larger boobs will give you that extra boost in self-esteem, but it won't. You'll soon find something else that you don't like about yourself. Instead of focusing on what you see as flaws, find the beauty inside of yourself. It's there, trust me!

I know that this is a touchy subject, but I'm going to drive home my point. Understand this: When you feel good on the inside, your beauty will shine through. Embrace your body just how it is.

Men, in society's eyes, you're lucky if you're tall, handsome, have a ripped body, and if you're successful too. If you have all of this, then you're viewed as the "cream of the crop," but I'm going to make an eye-opening point.

What about if you're a short man, how are you viewed? Do people tease you about having a "short-man's complex?" You probably feel intimidated when you're standing next to a tall man. Not because you're scared of him, but simply because the taller man is looked at as more of a man. Is it hard for you to find women that will go out on dates with you? Have you heard the dreaded saying, "You're nice and all, but you're just too short?" Or have you ever tried out for a sport and you get the dirty looks because nobody wants you on their team?

People really need to stop allowing body image to be so powerful. We are ALL different. Who are you to tell me what makes the "perfect body?" It's important to be comfortable in your own skin. Don't allow what other people deem to be perfect to get in the way of you loving yourself just the way you are. You are beautiful! You are handsome!

Embrace who you are. Learn to appreciate you for who you are. Embrace every unique thing about yourself. There's only "1" you! Love yourself! Take care of yourself!

Do You Know Your Self-Worth

Have you ever asked yourself that question? All of us should know the answer to that question. If you don't, it's time that you find out.

Ask yourself some questions, and then write down your answers and take a look at how you feel about yourself. Ask yourself questions like: Do I have a loving heart or is it cold and hardened? Do I care for others or am I selfish? Do I have a pleasant personality or am I mean? Am I sincere or do I put up a front knowing that I'm being phony? Am I optimistic or do I see negativity in everything? Am I a happy and content person or Am I grumpy and nobody likes to be around me? Am I faithful or do I take pleasure in cheating on others? Am I ambitious or do I lack drive and motivation?

There are so many questions that you can ask yourself. You can tailor the questions so that they'll fit your life style. The point that I'm trying to make is this: Get to know who you are and you will find your self-worth. I hope you took notice that I didn't name any material things. I want you to know your self-worth by who YOU are as a person.

"Things" don't have anything to do with who you are. You may have to take a little more time to think on that. I want you to search deep in your soul when you're asking yourself these questions. Block out all of the possessions that you have. Ask yourself what you see. Without all of the "bells and whistles," who are you REALLY? Are you okay with what you see? Ask yourself this question: If I didn't have all of the possessions that I have, how would I feel on the inside?

Don't be Afraid to Shine

How many people do you know that have various gifts
and talents that they don't pursue? You could be one of
these people. Deep down inside of you, you know that you
have a "special gift." However, you make every excuse in
the book not to act upon it. Here are a few examples that
I want you to take a look at. Change your mindset for a
brighter future.

Let's say that you love to sing, but people say
things like "You need to stop, you know you can't sing,"
and they jokingly tease you and make fun of you. Some
people can break down our self-esteem and they don't
even know it. In return, we start to doubt our abilities and
never give it a try. Look at it from this perspective. If you
LOVE to sing, go for it! You'll never know who's
searching for somebody with a unique voice such as
yours. Your voice may not sound good to the people that
you're singing in front of, but it may grab the attention of
somebody who's looking for something different. Ask
yourself this: What is a "good voice?" Everybody has a
different sound. That's what makes music so special. Your
raspy voice, extra deep voice, high-pitched voice, or soft
and sweet voice, may be just what they're looking for.
Don't be afraid to try. You don't want to live with the
regret that you never gave it a try. You'll never know how
great you could have been if you don't give yourself a

chance. Block out all of the negative comments that people have made and pursue your dreams. Sing with your heart. Sing with your soul. Sing with no fear. Sing your song. SING YOUR SONG! Don't be afraid to shine!

Let's say that you enjoy working with young adults in your community, but you're unable to obtain a good position because you're lacking the degree that is required. Instead of settling for jobs that don't allow you to utilize your natural born ability to motivate, stimulate, communicate, and overall impact the lives of our next generation, make a plan for yourself. Don't allow any negativity to set in. Go to school and meet with a counselor to discuss your goals and desires, and together you can work out a plan to get yourself to where you want to be. In the meantime, volunteer in your community. You may not be getting paid, but you're doing what you LOVE to do, and you're working on your degree at the same time. How awesome is that?! There's a great need for people that have passion, desire, and drive for what they do. It's okay to shine. Shine bright!

Fear

Let me first start out by saying that fear will cripple you. It will cause you to lose out on opportunities that are right in front of your face. Fear will cause self-doubt in whatever you're setting out to do. It will speak to you loudly, saying things like: "You'll fail. You're not good enough. What a silly idea, it won't go anywhere. You're wasting your time, it'll never work," etc.

Fear will cause you to miss out on your purpose in life. And if you're not careful, fear will steal everything that God intended for you to have. Fear is like a monster in the dark. It comes out to scare you and take control over your mind, body, and soul.

There's nothing positive about fear, and nothing good will ever come out of it. Erase fear from your vocabulary. Don't allow fear to take over your thinking. No matter what has taken place in your life as a child, teenager, or adult, you are BIGGER than fear.

Say it, believe it, live it. Transition your mindset to think positively. Of course it will take time, but as with anything, if you keep at it, it will become a habit. Fear has no place in our lives. It robs us of everything that's meant to be ours.

You're in Heaven, But I'm Living in Hell

I wanted to write a passage about losing your loved ones or having somebody close to you pass away, and you haven't quite gotten over it.

You're in heaven, but I'm living in hell because I can't seem to shake the horrible things that I said to you before you passed away. I didn't mean what I said, but you'll never know that because I waited too late to tell you. When I finally came to my senses and I called to apologize, I was told that you never woke up from your afternoon nap. I must admit, I said some pretty cruel things to you and I was totally out of line. I don't know how I'll ever get over the fact that I made you cry. I now live with the guilt that maybe I caused your death by all the stress that I brought on you. Mom, I know you're gone, but I'm so terribly sorry. I don't know what I'm going to do. My soul left me the day that I lost you. I might as well be in heaven with you. I wish that you were here so that I could hug you and tell you how much I'm sorry about what I said. My dear mom, I'm so sorry!

You're in heaven, but I'm living in hell because I just wouldn't listen and take directions. When I called home from the county jail, I was told that my grandmother had passed away. The pain and hurt that I felt was unexplainable. My grandmother used to warn me that my bad actions would catch up with me some day, but I chose not to listen. Her funeral is next week but, unfortunately, I won't get to say good bye because I'm locked up in jail. My heart feels like a heavy boulder. I'm devastated that I've lost the one person that cared about me. Why didn't I listen to the one woman that always showed me love? All she wanted was the very best for me. Did she know how much I loved her? I know that I caused her a lot of shame, and way too much pain. She was my favorite lady in the world. She was beautiful inside and out. Oh grandma, I can't take this pain! I won't ever be able to see your face again. I didn't listen and I didn't want to change my ways, so now I'm stuck in this jail cell mourning over the only woman who ever loved me. Why didn't I listen?

You're in heaven, but I'm living in hell because I let my attitude get the best of me and we hadn't spoken in years. As I was on my way to work, I received a phone call from my dad telling me that my sister was killed in a head on collision. My heart felt like it stopped beating for a long time. I couldn't feel my legs and, before I knew it, my whole body went numb. My sister and I hadn't spoken to one another in 8 years. Our last conversation resulted in an argument because I felt like she was trying to control my life. As I look back, she'd always been like that. She was only trying to protect me from the bad relationship that I was in. I remember that before hanging up the phone, I had told her how much I hated her and that I never wanted to speak to her again. That was 8 years ago. Now I get a phone call telling me that I'll never see my sister again. How can I live with what I've done? She tried calling me on numerous occasions, but I refused to speak to her. How could I be so stubborn when she only wanted the best for me? I loved my sister, yes I did! She'll never know how much, because she's never coming back again. It's too late. I would give anything to turn back the hands of time. Just to tell her how much I love her and that she was right. It's so sad that a fatal car accident is what it took to wake me up. I've learned a valuable lesson, but it's a little too late to make things right between my sister and I. She's in heaven now resting peacefully.

I thought it was important for me to write a passage like this for my book. I know it's painful, but you have to forgive yourself, you have to. I know it's hurtful when a loved one or someone close to you passes away. In order for you to have peace, you have to be able to forgive yourself.

We all make mistakes and sometimes we make horrible mistakes, but you have to forgive yourself in order to live in peace. God knows our hearts better than we do. If you ask for forgiveness, he will forgive you. If God can forgive us for what we've done, you have to forgive yourself too. If you don't, you'll feel tortured on the inside. That's why I named this passage, "You're in heaven, but I'm living in hell." You're living in hell in your mind because you won't let go of the mistakes you've made. In your mind, you keep going back to that painful day.

You've got to push forward, look forward, and don't look back. Do it for you!

Your Mask

People wear masks every day. What "Mask" you may ask? I like to refer to it as your "pretend face."

People can be going through pure hell in their lives, but they've become a pro at smiling through it all. They maintain a pleasant demeanor without anyone knowing what's really going on. Some people are being physically abused, and yet, when other people are around, they manage to make everything appear to be perfect. Many people are unhappy in their marriages but, when it's time for a gathering, they know how to put on a phony demeanor. They smile, laugh, and act as if nothing's wrong.

Okay, let's take a look at you. You've always been a smart student, you're attractive, everybody likes you, and you're an all-around great athlete. If they only knew the dirty little secrets that you've managed to hide so well.

And what about you, yeah you. You have a high power job, and you're an upright citizen, so they think. You're well-known in your community and everybody looks up to you. If they could only see what goes on in your mind. If they only knew the skeletons that you have in your "closet." You've been able to keep everybody in the dark about your sick fetish.

There are children that are being mistreated behind closed doors, but they've been warned to not say anything "or else." What about that family secret that you hide so well? Everybody thinks that you come from the perfect family. Parents, what about that child of yours? You're scared of them and afraid to say anything because you don't want to be embarrassed or judged.

I'm talking about, "THE MASK." Do you wear one? Many people do. What's in your closet? You have to take the mask off and deal with your issues head-on. Put your "pretend face" behind you. Step up and be bold. Face your demons once and for all. You've got to do it! You're problems won't just go away on their own. They'll be right there waiting to keep you hostage. Set yourself free today!

You Say You Love Me

As I struggle to get up from the floor, you look at me and say you didn't mean to do it and that you love me. My eyes are blackened from the punches you threw at me, my ribs feel broken and I'm in so much pain, my head is throbbing and aching because of the hard objects you so easily hit me with. And yet you still look me in my eyes and say you love me, BUT, I made you angry.

I can never do anything right in your eyes. You make it very clear that I'm nothing without you and nobody will ever want me. You speak to me badly all the time, beating my self-esteem further and further into the ground. You don't allow me to have any friends because you say they don't mean me any good. REALLY, I think to myself, and you do? I'm not allowed to see my family because you don't care too much for them.

You control me. I've given you power over me. I know it's wrong, but I don't have the strength to leave. I allow you to mentally, physically, and emotionally abuse me. I've become accustomed to being treated this way. I don't know any other life but you. The funny thing about it is, although you're mean to me and you degrade me, I still love you. I often ask myself, "How can you love someone who treats you this way?" If I had to use one word to describe you it would be EVIL. I'm in love with you and I don't know why. Maybe I want to believe you when you say "I love you."

I wrote this passage as a wakeup call for many individuals who experience abuse in their relationships. Love is NOT hurt and pain. Love is not being controlling, jealous, or easily angered. Love is not PAIN! Love is NOT PAIN!

YES

Are you one of those people that say "Yes" to everything and you find it hard to say "No?" Many people are dealing with the exact same thing.

Let me share something with you. That's not a healthy way of living. If you continue to live life saying "yes" all of the time, you will eventually get overwhelmed. I challenge you to try something different. The next time that somebody asks you if they can borrow some money, it's okay to say "I'm sorry, not this time," even if you do have the money. You have a right to say no. You shouldn't live life feeling obligated to do whatever another person asks you to do. You don't want to be known or labeled as a "YES" person.

Now, don't get me wrong, if you WANT to do it, then that's your choice. It's not healthy to do something because you feel obligated or pressured to do it, or because you're wondering if they'll be mad at you for saying no.

OKAY, lets' take a look at some of the things that people ask you do to: "Can you babysit for me? Can you come and pick me up and take me to the store? Can I come and live with you until I get back on my feet? Can I borrow your car? Can I borrow some money? Can I borrow your clothes?" Etc. It's always nice to do good deeds, but don't allow people to take advantage of your kindness.

I would recommend that you take the time to think about what they're asking you to do before you give an answer. It's okay to say, "Let me get back with you on that." Make sure that you follow up with the person even if the answer is no.

Here's a very important point that I would like to make: Don't feel like you have to explain yourself. Let your YES be yes and your NO be no. Say what you mean and mean what you say. Don't feel guilty because you chose to say "No" this time. You have that right. Don't allow anybody to make you feel bad for your decisions.

You Want a Baby, But are You Ready

People are so quick to say that they want a baby. But, do you know what it takes to raise a baby? It takes dedication, compassion, love and commitment.

When you decide to bring a baby into this world, YOU are no longer first, your baby is. So therefore, you have to be willing to be committed and dedicated to do what you have to do in order for your baby or babies to have a fair chance at having a good upbringing. Ask yourself some important questions: Do you like to sleep in and don't like getting up early or throughout the night? Do you still love to party and stay out late? Do you enjoy doing drugs and alcohol? Do you have a lot of random people coming in and out of your home at all times of the day and night? Are you lazy and don't like to clean or cook? Are you one of those people that don't have a job and you're not planning on working either?

Does crying irritate you? Would you have a problem with changing dirty diapers, cleaning up spit and vomit, and staying up late if you're little one becomes sick? Do you have the patience to teach them how to hold their bottle or eat on their own when they get to that certain stage? What about when it's time to teach them how to walk? I hope you understand that there's potty training that comes along with raising a child as well. Children have to go to the doctors to get their shots and checkups and, when they get a little older, you're responsible for taking them to the dentist too.

There are SO many things that come with raising a child, please understand this. It's not all fun and games. I can't tell you how many people I've heard saying, "I can't wait to dress my little one in cute clothes." REALLY, that's it? Reality check! Dressing kids in cute clothes is at the bottom of the list, and depending on the age of the child, you'll have to change their clothes several times a day. God forbid if you have a child that's sickly. You're going to have to have the compassion, strength, and love to nurture them through. It's not promised that your child will be healthy. Many women have complications that are unforeseen.

So, does having a child before you're ready sound fun now? I don't think so. Make sure that you're ready to be a parent before you decide to bring a precious child into this world. It wouldn't be fair to them if you're not.

Think it through carefully. Having a child is NOT a game. It's a very serious decision that you're going to have to make. Make sure that you're prepared to put them first. You're children should not come second to what you still want to do.

Childhood

So, what kind of childhood did you have? It's important that you are willing to be open, honest, and dig deep for your truth.

Is hugging uncomfortable for you because you never received hugs as a child? Do you still suffer from anger issues because you were picked on all of the time? Is it hard for you to trust others because you were taken advantage of as a child? Do you find it hard to sleep at night because you never knew who was going to come into your room? Do you find it hard to let people inside of your space because, when you were young, all people did was hurt you and cause you pain? Are you a nervous person because you never knew what was going to happen to you on a daily basis? Do you have problems communicating because, as a child, you were told to shut up and do what you were told, because you didn't have a voice and your opinions didn't matter? Does being around people who are getting sloppy drunk bring back horrible flashbacks?

What about the person who raised you? Does the thought of their presence send chills up your spine because they were so unfair and mean to you? Did those beatings you used to get affect the way that you raised your kids? Does it affect how you are in relationships? Do you suffer from low self-esteem because you were always put down? Do you hold resentments because you weren't raised by one or both parents? Are you living with anger everyday because you didn't have a good childhood at all? All you knew was hurt, pain, and disappointment. No child should've gone through and experienced what you did.

Let me first start out by saying, you made it! Although things were rough and unfair for you, you were able to push through and survive it. I know you may still be dealing with what happened to you in your childhood, but don't allow it to consume you. Don't allow what happened in the past affect the present. Give yourself a fighting chance. Allow yourself to be free. Give yourself peace within and be happy. You can't change what happened in the past, but you can change your future.

Let your faith heal and strengthen you. It may be hard, but you also have to forgive the person or people that hurt you. Forgiveness is necessary for you to be able to heal. It will clear your mind and keep you from being bound to the negative things that happened to you in the past. Leave the past behind you and be in peace. I know that it hurts, and I know that it's unfair. I know that what they did almost ruined your life or did ruin your life. I know it's hard. But do it for you! You are somebody! Everybody has a story. Everybody has a past. Everybody has a good or a bad ending. Don't allow your past to rob you and keep you in darkness. Press forward and stay hopeful for a brighter future.

How Confident are You

Would you still be confident if you didn't wear makeup? Would you still feel confident if you took off your contacts, fake eye lashes, and didn't have those fillers in your lips? Would you still be confident if you didn't have breast implants? Would you still be confident if you didn't get that liposuction? Would you still be confident if you didn't have your wigs, extensions, and weaves to wear? Would you still be confident if you could no longer afford to get your French manicures, Acrylic nails, Silk wraps and all of the other services that nail salons offer? Would you still feel good about yourself if you couldn't afford to wear name-brand clothes?

How would you feel if you were used to living in a beautiful home in a high-class neighborhood and had to be reduced to living in an apartment? If you didn't drive a top-of-the-line car, would you still feel like you're "the man/woman?" If you didn't have a job making a lot of money and you had to work for minimum wage, could you still hold your head up high and feel good about yourself? If you weren't in a position where you could go anywhere you wanted to at any time, would you still feel like you're living "the life?" If you had to give up all of your fancy things, would you still be confident if you were left with the basics?

Most people say that they're confident, but they have no idea. If you didn't have everything that you have, would people still want to associate with you? Would you have a lot of friends? Do the people you associate with like you for who you are, or do they like what you can offer them? Ask yourself this question and be honest with yourself: Am I REALLY confident, or do THINGS make me feel confident?

Finish STRONG

So, you've decided to finally muster up enough courage to do what you've wanted to do for a long time now. And here comes that negative voice inside your head saying, "You'll never finish. You always give up too soon." Your heart says "You can do it!" but your mind says "You'll fail." The battle between the mind and the heart can be very frustrating.

Aren't you tired of starting something and giving up before you can see the final results? Ask yourself: Why do I start something and can't ever finish it? Am I afraid of success? Am I afraid of failure? Or could it be that I don't believe in myself enough? There can be all kinds of reasons why you don't follow through on what you set out to do. Aren't you tired of feeling and being defeated?

Push through those negative feelings no matter what that negative voice inside your head tells you. If you have a vision or a plan, don't stop until you get to the end. God has NOT given us a spirit of fear. Dig deep down inside of you and find the strength to carry on. Don't give up! Continue to fight to the end. You can do it! You will do it! You are doing it!

Keep your head up and be encouraged. Don't give up on yourself and don't give up on your dreams. FINISH STRONG and believe! BELIEVE in yourself! Imagine the feeling you will feel once you get to the end. You will feel a GREAT sense of accomplishment. Giving up is simply not an option for you!

You Never Know

"Honey, I'll be right back. I'm going to the store to pick up some things for the house." But he/she never comes back because they were hit and killed by a drunk driver. You never know!

"I love you mom and dad. I'll see you after school." But you don't ever get the chance to see your child again because some idiot decided to come and shoot up the school. You never know!

"Hey you! I'm on my way. I should be there in about an hour." But your friend never makes it because somebody carjacked them and then killed him/her. You never know!

"Hey Sis! My plane should be landing in 20 minutes. I can't wait to see you!" But before the landing, something goes wrong and the plane goes down. You never know!

"Hi Grandma. I'm coming by to visit you next Thursday. I can't wait to see your beautiful smile." But, unfortunately, your grandmother passes away unexpectedly. You never know!

"Good morning Grandpa! I can't wait for you see me play in my first game this weekend." But your grandpa never makes it because somebody robbed him at gun point as he was leaving his home. You never know!

"Hello my dear Aunt! My friends and I can't wait to have dinner at your house tonight." But you never get a chance to have that dinner because her ex-boyfriend decided to come over unexpectedly and shoot her. You never know!

"Hey big brother! I can't wait to see the new office at your job." But you never get the chance to see him because a co-worker went off and killed everybody at the work site. You never know!

"Hello cousin! I was calling to ask you if you wanted to meet up at the park for a picnic today." But the picnic never takes place because your cousin was jumped and beat up due to a gang mistaking him for the wrong person while he was waiting for you to show up. You never know!

These are just SOME of the examples of the hurt and pain that people go through on a daily basis. We never see it coming. That's why I can't stress it enough. LOVE, APPRECIATE, and VALUE your family, friends, and the people that are close to you. You never know!

Be Careful what You Wish on Others

Be mindful and careful of what you say about people. Be extra careful of what you wish upon people, because it can be reversed and end up happening to you. You might not believe this, but I've heard people say things like: "I hope they lose their home. I hope they lose their good job. I hope their spouse leaves them," and all other sorts of ugly things.

Speaking negatively about somebody and wishing that ill things will happen to them is just plain ugly. You better watch it! You'll find yourself in that same predicament that you were wishing upon them. Why would you want to wish bad things on somebody anyways? What does that say about you? It's not a good look, and thinking ill thoughts like that will corrupt your spirit.

Fill your spirit with good thoughts. Don't focus on what others have and what they're doing. For example, if someone is driving a car that you really want, don't say or think to yourself "I hope they lose their car." Instead, fill your mind with good thoughts. Try changing your mindset to say things like "I pray that one day I can afford to drive a car like that." See, doesn't that sound way nicer? No need to be jealous and envious of what others have. You may say that it's not jealousy, but why else would you want to see somebody lose their things?

Be honest with yourself. We should all learn how to rejoice when others are doing well. In due time, you will get the things that you desire. But, in the meantime, keep your mind clear of unhealthy thoughts.

Don't be in a Rush

I want you to take a close look at your life. Do you find yourself rushing all of the time?

Well, Think about THIS: We go about living our lives on a daily basis, and we have what we call a "to-do list." We have to do grocery shopping, stop by the cleaners, pick our children up from day care/school, wash the car, walk and feed the pets, go by the bank. And the list goes on and on.

Every day we do what would be considered "the norm." We get SO busy that sometimes we forget to slow down and appreciate life as it should be. Don't get me wrong, all of these things that we do are important, but it's also equally important to find a good balance with everything else in our lives. Learn to relax. Don't be in a rush. Take your time, and remember to value the things that are truly important. Many people don't realize just how valuable life is until something tragic happens. I'm going to give you an eye-opening example of what I'm talking about.

Do you take the time to hug and/or kiss your loved ones every day? Do you take the time to cook and then sit down with the family to enjoy it? Do you take time out of your day to just laugh, smile, or unwind from it all? Do you make time for "family time?" Do you take the time to ask your mate or somebody who's close to you "How was your day" and be patient enough to allow them to answer and then talk about it? Do you take the time to say "I love you?" Do you take the time to sit down and have long, deep conversations? Do you allow yourself time to do what you enjoy, or do you spend all of your time only doing what you HAVE to do? Can you sit through an entire movie or show without answering or looking at your phone? Are you too busy on the computer that you don't even notice what's really going on in your household? Do you allow your mind to take a break and rest? Did you stop doing something that you love because you feel like you're too old? Remember, age is just a number. When was the last time, or have you ever taken a long train ride and enjoyed the sound, sights, and people around you?

I could go on and on, but I think that you get my point by now. We have to allow time for the things that really matter. Now that I've got your attention, it's time for you to ask yourself: "What can I do to bring balance into my life?" When we know better, we should do better. You owe it to yourself. Live life to the fullest! Value what's most important, and allow yourself to enjoy all of the peace that comes with it.

Get it Together People

So, you go to church every Sunday, you attend bible study throughout the week, and you may even be active within your church, but what does all of that mean?

Some people think that because they go to church regularly, that makes them better than the next person. I think not! Going to church doesn't make you a "good person." Anybody can get dressed up, go to church, and pretend.

It's what's in your heart. What is your heart filled with? What kind of person are you towards others? Do you go to church just for show? Do you attend church because that's how you were raised and it's the "right thing" to do? People attend church for many different reasons, but the people who really get me are the ones that think that they're "holier than thou." They are so judgmental and they find fault in everybody else when they're huge hypocrites themselves. God looks at what's in our hearts, not how much we attend church.

Ask yourself a few questions: Do you have love in your heart? Do you care for other people? Are you a giver and enjoy helping others, or are you selfish? Do you have self- control or are you easily angered and have no patience? Are you kind or rude toward others? Do you have peace and joy within, or are you so full of anger that nobody likes to be around you?

Get it together my church-going people. Just because you go to church doesn't mean that you're better than anybody else. I challenge you to look deep within yourselves. Do you like what you see or could you be a better person? You know the truth, but are you willing to change?

The next time that you want to judge somebody else, take a good look at yourself. Are you free from sin? Instead of looking down on others and talking about them, pray for them and lift them up. I'm sure that when God found you, you were a HOT MESS. Show some compassion for others instead of beating them further down into the ground.

We've got to do better. Way better! God is LOVE!

Worrying is Just not Worth it

We have all experienced it at some point in our lives, Worrying.

I want to break down why worrying is just not worth it. Worrying causes one to feel tormented, anxious, sick, moody, and irritated. It causes one to over eat or not eat at all, have disturbing thoughts, feel pain in your body, and have sleepless nights. The feeling of worthlessness will soon take over you before you know it. Please don't underestimate what worrying can do. Depending on the severity of what you're worrying about, worrying will put you in a place where you're unable to function in life and want to give up on living altogether. Worrying is when you let your mind take over. When you worry, your mind is literally all over the place. Worrying, without a doubt, will rob you of your peace of mind.

I want to discuss ways that we can minimize worrying so that it won't negatively impact our lives. We have to first accept the fact that, when we've done all that we can do, we have to let it go. I know that letting go of a situation may seem tough, but remember all of the things that I discussed in the first paragraph. We can't afford to ignore what worrying does to us. Letting go doesn't mean that you're giving up, it means that you've accepted a situation for what it is. Some of you may say that it's easier said than done, but you have to realize just how dangerous worrying can be in our lives.

It's a hard pill to swallow, but some things we JUST can't change. We can, however, change our way of thinking so that it won't bring permanent damage to our lives. Half of the time we worry about things that will eventually work themselves out in their own timing.

What I truly want you to get out of this passage is that we can't change people, places or things. We CAN'T change people. We CAN'T change places. We CAN'T change things. Meditate on that for a while. It will definitely help you push forward once you clearly understand this.

Instead of worrying, pray and ask for strength, courage, and understanding to deal with the situation in a positive manner, no matter what the circumstances are. Worrying is just not worth it.

The Words You Spoke to Me

The words you spoke to me hurt my heart so badly. Why did you say what you said to me? Did you mean to cause me this much pain?

Have you ever had somebody say something to you and it literally hurt you to the core? I'm sure that most of us have had this happen in some part of our lives. Whether it was done by someone on the job, a family member, a significant-other, our children, close friends, or a stranger, words really do hurt.

We have to be careful with what comes out of our mouths, especially when we're upset. Once your words are spoken, unfortunately, you can't take them back. You can later apologize, and the person may forgive you, but we have to grow up and be mature enough to be quiet when we can't say anything nice. We have to learn self-control with our words. Some words that we speak can damage people in a way that we never thought was possible. Some words we speak can strip away someone's self-esteem. Some words we speak can cause one to take their life. Some words we speak can literally make one become ill.

Words can hurt so badly. We really need to understand that, and change what we say. Be careful of what comes out of your mouth. It's time to take ownership for "SELF." No more excuses for your immature and insensitive behavior.

Prejudices and Stereotypes

I can only imagine how many good relationships we pass up because of prejudices and stereotypes.

People can be so judgmental and not even give you a chance because of the color of your skin. What does skin color have to do with anything? We're all people.

Be honest with yourself. Have you ever been wrong about a person before you took the time to get to know them? I'm sure you answered yes. How many of you grew up in a family where talking badly about another race was okay? Are you guilty of not wanting to sit next to a person because of the color of their skin? Have you ever wanted to be friends with another person of a different race, but you didn't know how it would look to your family and friends?

Let's talk about stereotypes. So, some of you believe that ALL black people are good at sports. Well that's simply not true. My daughter couldn't play sports to save her life. I tell her all of the time "Stick to dancing honey, stick to dancing." Some people will argue that men are stronger than women. They supposedly work harder than we do, they're smarter, and they can handle stress better than women can. Well, we all know that's not a fact. Some men are lazy, ignorant, can't handle pressure, don't have any backbone, can't take up for themselves, don't have a job, and they don't want one either. What about the labels that some people put on Mexicans? They will work hard for little pay, they're dirty, and most of them are over here illegally. Supposedly Arabs and Muslims are all terrorists and they can't be trusted. Asians are really good at math. All Irish people love to drink and they're all drunks. Blondes are unintelligent.

Do you see how ignorant all of these examples sound? We all have a right to our own opinions, but this is just plain wrong! I don't want to be judged and we shouldn't judge others until we get to know them personally. If you don't take the time to get to know somebody for yourself, but you choose to pass judgment anyways, then you need to take a good look at yourself. It's wrong and there's no other way of looking at it.

Why ME

We have ALL asked that question before. We as humans don't understand why we have to go through certain things in life. I don't think that anybody could actually say that they enjoy going through trying times. Difficult times will bring out our true character. It's not until you're going through something difficult that you see just how strong or weak that you really are.

With some things that we experience in life, we don't understand why they happen to us. It just doesn't seem fair that we're going through this. We think: "Why did I have to lose MY child? Why did I have to lose my job? Why did I have to become ill? Why did I have to lose my home? Why did I have to get in a car accident and lose everything? Why did I have to be born into a family that doesn't love me? Why did I have to be violated? Why did I live a life filled with drugs and alcohol? Why did I NOT succeed in life? Why did I end up going in and out of jail?" WHY, WHY, WHY?

There are a ton of other things that people ask "WHY" about. These things don't feel good and you probably wished that they never happened.

Although we may have experienced unpleasant things in our lives, we can't afford to give up the fight for our lives. Allow God to heal your every hurt and pain. He says in Hebrews 13:5 that he will "Never leave nor forsake us." His word also says in Matthew 11:28 "Come unto me, all ye that labour and are heavy laden, and I will give you rest." What He is saying is: "Come to me, you don't have to go through this alone. I will give you complete peace in the midst of the situation. I will heal and set you free. I will carry the pain for you." God is a good God! He loves and cares for us.

Don't try to do this alone. Allow him to come in your heart and heal you. AMEN!

We Need Order

Many people struggle with having and maintaining order in their lives.

Here are some examples: You're always late paying bills. You're always running late to work or any kind of appointment. You're forgetful all of the time. You're spending money that you don't really have. You're driving cars and living in a home that you know you can't afford. You're spending and using up all of your savings just to keep up with other people. You're spending money on cigarettes and lotto tickets, but there's no food in the home for your kids. You're buying that new suit just to look good at the party, but you're behind on your bills. You're spending $200 on the newest Jordon's, but you're kids don't have descent school clothes. You're taking that trip out of town, but you don't know how you're going to get back. You're spending money on all of the latest name-brand items that you can find, and yet you complain that you can't ever save any money.

There's literally a long list of things that I could name, but I think you get the picture. There's no doubt about it, we need order in our lives. Do you have order in your life, or are you all over the place? That's not a healthy way of living. It's important to have a good balance in your life. If you're making irresponsible choices, you'll always be off balance somewhere in your life.

The things I've named above are just SOME of the irresponsible things that people do. What does your lifestyle say about you? Do you live without any order, or are you responsible? What changes can you make today to bring order and direction into your life?

Be Cautious who You have Children By

Before you make the choice to have children, make sure that you choose wisely about who you have them by. This passage is not just for women. Men, it's important for you to really think about what kind of woman that you want to raise your children.

Here are some things to consider: What kind of character does the person you're considering to have children by have? Is he/she stable? Does your partner have addictions that can affect raising your child in a healthy environment or cause birth defects with the baby? Does he/she have health issues that are a concern? Is he/she in DEBT? Is your mate responsible and dependable? Will he/she set good examples for your children? In other words, will they be a good role model? What about morals and values? Do you share the same ones or will they clash? Do you equally want to have a child? This is the most important question that you should be asking yourselves. Make sure that you're both on the same page. Do you both work and have you both discussed how you're going to take care of the child/children? Have you both discussed how much it will cost to bring a child into the world? It's important to know these things. Having children can be very expensive. You have to have a plan in place and know what you'll need to do to fully be able to provide for your child. What kind of family does your mate come from? Ask yourself this: If you both decided that you didn't want to be together anymore, would both of you be mature and still take care of your responsibility or will you bail out? That's why it's important to know the character of the person that you're choosing to have a baby by. Character says a lot about a person. Pay attention.

Take your emotions out of the picture and really look at the person you're considering. What do you see? Seriously, what do you see? Some people choose to have children by people who have no business having children. The signs are there, but they're swept under the rug. For the most part, what you see is what you're gonna get. Having a child won't make things better and it won't make someone change. I hope that this passage has opened up your eyes and given you insight. Make the right choice and be wise.

Giving

If you're a giver, then you know firsthand what it feels like to make a difference in somebody's life. There's nothing like bringing a smile to somebody's face and making them feel special.

What a blessing it is to be able to feed a family that's in need. What a blessing it is to give clothes to a person to help them stay warm. What a blessing it is to give money to people that don't have it. What a blessing it is to give a person a warm place to stay. What a blessing it is to give a ride to a person who has no other means of transportation.

What a blessing it is to give them something that doesn't cost a thing. I'm talking about a smile, a hand shake, a hug, your time, and conversation. You'd be surprised by how many people would just appreciate your time and kindness. I've tried on many occasions to give people money who I know needed it, but they refused to accept it. They would rather talk to me and have a conversation. Not everybody wants a hand out. They may be down on their luck, but what they sometimes want is the acknowledgement that they're human too. Some people have a fall in their lives and can never make it back. Some people go through something tragic in their lives that send them to the streets. Some people are out on the streets because their mind is gone. Other people simply like the street life. Whatever the case may be, they belong to somebody. They all have families. Somebody out there loves them.

When it comes to giving, don't just think about giving money. Sometimes giving can just be your time. It's so easy to give somebody a few dollars. Try making a difference in somebody's life by giving them encouraging words. Speak positive things into their lives. There's a joy in giving. Be mindful that there are so many ways that we can give. It's a blessing to be a blessing to others.

How do we get Past This

How do we get past the pain that we've caused each other? We've both done hurtful things to one another. Can we get past this? Is our love worth fighting for? We've both invested so much time into this relationship, so it's not easy to walk away. What about all of the memories that we've created? Do we throw it all away and act as if this never happened? How do we get past this, the hurt and the pain? We both blame each other and it gets us nowhere. It's hard for us to communicate because we don't listen to what the other person has to say. How do we get past this? All of the arguing and fighting needs to stop. How will we ever be able to move forward if we don't see what we've both done? The "blame game" has gotten old.

Can we just move forward and forgive? Can we just let what happened in the past stay in the past? We've both done wrong and we're both at fault. We both allowed ourselves to be persuaded by someone else on the outside. We both made a choice to do what we did. We can't change that. How do we get past this? If this relationship is truly meant to be, we both have to grow up and deal with what we've created in our relationship. We're both at fault, completely at fault. I can't believe that the temptation got to us. We both knew better, but we both made a choice. Now we both have to live with this choice.

How do we get past this? We ask for forgiveness, we forgive, we pray that God will heal our hearts, and slowly build up our trust again. Is that enough? Will we be able to make it through? Only God knows, but I'm willing to give it a try. Are you willing?

I Don't Know, I Just Don't Like Her

How is it that you don't like me and you don't really know me? I see the way that you look at me, and it's obvious that you dislike me.

You say that I'm stuck-up and that I walk around like I'm better than you. You look me up and down as if there's something on me. You talk about me and you speak lies. You don't like the way I dress. Nope, not stylish enough for you. You hate me because I'm not big on wearing makeup. I don't like to gossip or put other people down, so that makes me stuck-up in your eyes. I'm intelligent, so you view me as a know-it-all. I'm not into drugs, alcohol or sleeping around, so I'm viewed as perfect. You can't stand the way that I speak. You say that I'm too proper. I set challenging goals for myself to ensure I'll have a great future, and you tell me "That's a lot. I doubt you'll accomplish that." I respect myself and others around me, so that makes me a "GOOD GIRL."

I understand that you just don't like me, but let me tell you a little bit about myself. I'm not stuck-up nor do I think that I'm better than anybody else. I was taught to walk like I have a purpose in life and keep my head held high because I AM somebody. I don't keep up with the latest fashion or buy everything new that comes out. I don't need to do that. Clothes don't make me who I am. For I know who I am as a woman. Material things don't define me. I choose not to wear makeup. I'm confident in my own skin and I feel beautiful without it. I don't need to gossip or put people down to feel big. In my eyes, that shows a lack of confidence and somebody that needs attention, but is going about it the wrong way. Intelligence is a beautiful gift and I won't compromise that for anybody. I won't destroy my temple with drugs and alcohol, for I know better than this, and I choose to make wise decisions. I choose not to sleep around. I respect my body too much for that. I'm saving my love for someone that's special, my husband. So, you say that I speak too properly?! What is "too proper?" I speak with purpose. I speak clearly. I know how to express my thoughts and opinions. I communicate effectively while holding eye contact. I don't need to use slang to get my point across.

My future is bright because I do right. If you fail to prepare, prepare to fail. I respect myself because I know my value. I respect others because I was raised with good morals and values. Keep on disliking me because you're clearly not on my level. I'm going places. I have peace. I love who I am, I am me.

I'm in Love With You

I love the way you look at me and smile. I can see in your eyes that you truly love me. The way you touch me is oh-so gentle, being careful not to be too rough with me. You're always respectful in front of other people and behind closed doors. You always ask me if you could be of any help when you see that I have a lot on my plate. We work very well as a team because we understand that we are "one." We both work hard to take care of our family, our household is important to the both of us. We don't put each other down, we help build each other up and support one another's dreams. When either one of us is feeling down, the other one knows just what to do.

We took the time to really get to know each other inside and out. We have fun with each other; we're both big kids at heart. We may argue sometimes, but we always apologize and make up promptly. We've grown and learned that we will have our differences. We communicate all of the time. We understand that we always have to be aware and be able to listen to one another. We also understand that communication is a MUST in any relationship. We BOTH do work around the house, simply because we are equal. We're consistent in showing our love. When you love somebody, that's what you're supposed to do. I'm in love with you for all of the right reasons.

Ask yourself, do you feel genuinely loved? If not, why not? If you're not getting the love that you deserve, it's time to go back to the drawing line. It's important to get to the bottom of why you aren't receiving that love. What went wrong? Was true love ever there? Were you in the relationship for all of the wrong reasons? Dig deep until you find the answer.

It's Okay to be Different

You've always known that you were different, but this has never quite sat right with you. You try to bend your personality to fit in with the others. You go out of your way to try to impress a complete stranger. You change the way that you dress to try to fit in with the rest of the crowd. You hang out in places that you're completely uncomfortable in. You open yourself up so freely even when you know that they really don't like you. You offer to pay for everything because you think that'll make people want to be your friend. You pretend that you're okay with what they're doing but, on the inside, you're totally against it. You do a lot of cussing in front of them, but you feel bad about it later because you were raised to be better than that. You always put up a front acting like you're tough, but you're actually very kind and loving. You don't enjoy going to clubs and bars, but you go anyways because that's what THEY like to do. You just want to fit in.

Why do we waste so much time and energy trying to be something that we're not? Why do some people find it so hard to just be themselves? Peer pressure doesn't just affect children and young adults. It affects grown-ups as well. We try our hardest to blend in with what is considered the "in-crowd," not realizing that what we're actually doing is being a follower. It's okay to be different.

78

Don't lower your standards and compromise what you believe in just to be around people that you think are cool. Be yourself! This world is filled with all kinds of people. If you're willing to be patient, you'll find friends that believe, respect, and value what you stand for, and they'll appreciate your friendship for what it is.

I Thought I Knew You, But I Was Wrong

Have you ever thought that you really knew somebody, and you came to realize that you didn't? It's not a good feeling is it? The betrayal you feel is unexplainable. Okay, let's take a look at some of the things that you or somebody that you know may have experienced in life.

I trusted you with my secret and you shared it to anybody that would listen. You promised me that you would love me and never leave me like the others did, but you did the exact same thing in the end. You said that you'd always have my back but, in the end, you ended up putting a knife so far deep in it. I was in so much disbelief. You said that I could trust you, but that was a lie. After spending so much time with you, I see that you were not to be trusted at all. You said that you'd be faithful and that you'd never cheat on me. Look at me now, single and alone, still hurting from the pain that you caused me.

You promised me that you'd marry me, but now you're marrying my best friend. You said that you didn't want kids, but I hear that you've settled down and you're raising 3 of your own. You told me that you weren't interested in the job that I was applying for, but you went behind my back, applied, and got the job that I wanted. I thought that you didn't know how to start up a business, but somehow you're running a successful business of your own now. You told me that I could always call you and that you'd always be there for me, but instead, you never picked up or called me back. I can't believe that all of this time I thought that you were very gifted and smart, but come to find out, you cheat and pay people to do your work. I thought that you worked hard for your money, but I know now that you're a hustler. You take pleasure in fooling people with your schemes and lies. I thought I knew you, but I didn't.

I tried to tackle a lot of things that people go through. I couldn't cover them all, but don't feel alone. We've all been there. We can only go by what people show us at the time. When you find out whom people truly are, you have some decisions to make. Don't stay and allow yourself to be a victim.

Give Me a Chance

Ladies: You say that you would like to meet a great guy
and that you want to settle down and be happy. The
problem is that some of you have too many stipulations,
and this could be the reason why you can't find what
you're looking for. Here are some examples of what I hear
some women say: "Girl, he has to be at least 6 feet tall. I
can't date a short man. He has to have a good job. If he
doesn't make as much money as I do, then he can keep on
walking. I don't want a man that doesn't have a nice
vehicle. I can't be seen in an old beat up car. He must
have his own home because I have mine. If he wants to be
with me, he has to spoil me. I like to look nice and I love
to travel," etc. Have you ever given thought to the idea
that your "prince charming" may not have any of the
things that you're demanding?

Men: I've heard some men say: "Man, she has to
be thick. I'm not into skinny girls. She's got to have some
meat. I need something that I can hold on to. Man, she's
got to have nice boobs. I can't have a woman with a flat
chest on my arm. She's got to have a pretty face. I can't be
dating somebody who doesn't turn heads. She needs to
have her own. I'm not trying to take care of a woman.
Man, I can't date a woman with kids. I'm not trying to be
a daddy to somebody else's kids." Men, please realize
this: Beauty is only skin deep. A pretty face only goes so

far. There's more to a woman than how thick she is, how pretty she is, how big her boobs are, etc.

The examples that I've shared with you above don't even come close to all of the "standards" that some people set. This was just a short illustration. It amazes me how we can eliminate people before we even give them a chance. Has it ever occurred to you that your soul-mate may not have everything that you're wishing for at first? You could be passing up the best thing that'll ever happen to you. You say that you're looking to settle down and meet that special person, right? Then you're going about it the wrong way. I also want to point this out: Just because someone doesn't have all of the things that you're wishing for doesn't mean that they aren't "the one."

I'm going to get personal for a minute. I've met men in the past that have had it all, but there was absolutely no chemistry between us. I didn't enjoy their company, they didn't communicate well, and they weren't any fun to be around. YES, they had a great career. YES, they drove a nice car. YES, they were handsome. YES, they had their own, but...they weren't for me. I personally like a man with a great personality because I'm very outgoing myself. I love a man that can communicate. I think that it's very attractive when a man is driven. I like a man that can be sensitive. I like a man that's confident, but not cocky. I like a man that's independent, has confidence, and can stand on his own. I like a man that's respectful. I like a man that's not afraid to show their feelings, etc.

That's why I married my husband. In case you didn't notice, I didn't mention anything about what he had. I gave examples of what characteristics drew me to him. It had nothing to do with how he looked, what he drove, where he lived, or what kind of money he made.

If you truly want to be happy in your life and you're searching for the right one, you have to open up your options. Stop being so CRITICAL about everything and open yourself up for true love.

So, the next time that somebody approaches you and you start a conversation, and you soon find out he/she doesn't live up to what you were expecting, get to know them from the inside first and then determine if they are worth your time. Don't allow what they don't have to be the final factor. Some people just need a chance.

I would like to get personal again for a minute. When I first met my husband, he didn't have anything near what I wanted him to have, but look at him now! I'm glad that I didn't pass him up. It just goes to show that, even though the person you meet may not have everything that you desire at the moment, it doesn't mean that they're not the right one for you. It will all work out and, in time, they will have what you desire. The final choice is yours. I hope that you think about this for a while. This is really good food-for-thought.

Focus on YOU

Instead of focusing on other people, learn to focus more on yourself.

Some people spend way too much time focusing on other peoples' problems and they don't even see how much mess is going on in their own personal lives. We can sometimes get caught up in who's cheating, who's getting fired from their job, who's losing their home, who's pregnant, who's getting a divorce, who's getting locked up, who's losing their vehicle, etc.

We need to turn a new chapter in our lives and focus on what REALLY matters. I challenge you to focus more on yourself and say goodbye to the negative energy that you've been allowing to take up most of your time. It's time to focus on YOU. It's time to get it together. It's time to go to a new level in your life. Let go of the drama in your life and focus on becoming a better person yourself.

The truth hurts sometimes doesn't it? Learn and grow from your shortcomings. Say NO to negativity and say YES to positivity. Negativity has no place in your life. It only takes away from you. Associate with people that bring out the best in you. Do not be deceived. Hanging around people who thrive off of negativity will eventually corrupt your spirit too. It's important to be wise and not allow people to dump all of that negative stuff into your spirit. Hang around people that are positive and uplifting. Live a life worth talking about and sharing with others. Let your light shine!

I'm not the One Who Hurt You

Have you or somebody that you know ever been so hurt that you built up a wall and now you won't let anybody in?

When people hurt us, it's normal to want to be more careful the next time around. BUT, being careful shouldn't put you in a position where you don't allow yourself to live again. Let me explain it to you this way. When you build up walls, you're being unfair to yourself. You're not allowing yourself to really live. Let's take a look at some of the things that you do.

Most likely, you're VERY guarded and you have an attitude when anybody shows you any kind of interest. If you do choose to open up, your conversations revolve around what you went through with the last person. If a person starts to get close to you, you'll find ways to make them back off. You make the current person pay for what the last person did to you. You have serious trust issues, so you question EVERYTHING. Let's be honest: Jealousy is now a big issue, AND, if he or she wanted to go out with their friends without you, they're sure to pay for it because you'll make it a point to do so.

I'm trying to get you to clearly see that, when you hold on to what the last person did to you, it will have a negative effect on your life. It will be extremely hard to move forward with your negative thought pattern. You may not even realize it, but now you've got the "ALL men/women are NO GOOD attitude." If you keep up that kind of attitude, you're shooting yourself in the foot for sure. You're not giving the person a fair chance. They're NOT the person that hurt you. It's important for you to remember that. If you DO find yourself interested in a person, look at THEIR actions. Don't focus on what the previous person did to you.

If you want to move forward, you have to learn how to trust again. You have to start somewhere. There's nothing wrong with being careful, that's being smart. If you're still hurt, confused, and angry, then take a break from dating. It's OK! Take time to heal.

I'm going to end on this note: When we open ourselves up, we don't know how things will turn out. We are taking a chance. Make sure that the person you're considering a relationship with is worth taking a chance for. Some of the people that we allow in our lives show us bad signs from the beginning and WE choose to ignore them. ~Think about it~

It's a Beautiful Day

Why is it a beautiful day, you may ask? It's a beautiful day because we woke up this morning. Some people didn't. It's a beautiful day because we have our health and strength. Some people are battling sickness or are in the hospital fighting for their lives. It's a beautiful day because we have legs to walk. Some people would give anything to walk again or to jog, ride a bike, skate, run, play tennis, ski, etc.

We have to be THANKFUL!

It's a beautiful day because we have eyes to see. Thank God for our eyesight because there's so much to take in from our surroundings. It's a beautiful day because we're in our right minds. Some people have lost their minds due to traumatic/hurtful events, mental health issues, and unfortunate accidents. It's a beautiful day because we can hear. Some people are deaf and wish that they could hear. Do you realize how important hearing is?

We ALL have so much to be thankful for. All we have to do is look around us and see how blessed that we really are.

For people who may be reading this that are battling any of the things that I mentioned above, make no mistake, you are still here for a reason. God doesn't make ANY mistakes. We may not always understand

WHY some things are the way that they are, but God has a reason for everything. I pray that God keeps you in his perfect peace.

Don't Make Decisions when You're Angry

Please don't make decisions when you're angry. No matter what you may think, you aren't thinking rationally when you're upset.

When we're angry, we tend to make bad decisions that we'll later regret. When you find yourself getting angry, take a deep breath. Ask yourself what you're angry about, what caused you to become so angry, and what you can do differently that will change the circumstances at hand to something positive. We need to practice self-control. If we can't control our ways of thinking, our behavior will get the best of us every time.

People have lost their lives from making decisions while they're angry. It's not worth it! Learn to channel your feelings in a positive way. We all know when we're starting to boil over. When you feel yourself getting to that point, if you can, remove yourself from the situation if you feel like it's going to get out of control. If you're forced to deal with the issue at hand at that time, remember what I stated above. Keep your composure and practice self-control.

You don't have a right to hit anybody just because you're angry. You don't have a right to say mean and evil things just because you're angry. You don't have a right to damage and ruin other people's things because you're angry. You don't have a right to act immaturely just because things aren't going your way.

It's time to grow up! Take control of yourself and make better decisions. Don't make decisions when you're angry. It can cost you your life.

I'm Staying for the Kids

I hear a lot of people say that they're staying in an unhappy relationship for the sake of the kids. Both parents clearly don't get along anymore and they both want to get out of the relationship.

This is where you have to ask yourself some tough questions: Is arguing and bickering in front of the kids all of the time healthy? Is it fair to the kids that they have to live in a home where we don't speak respectfully to one another? Is it fair that the kids have to witness abuse? Remember, abuse is not just physical. Is it fair that the kids hear us argue over finances all of the time? Is it fair to pretend that we're happy when they know that we're not? What kind of message are you sending to them?

When you're in a relationship and you're both willing to work things out, like going to counseling or getting outside help from the church or whatever your choice may be, that's one thing. But when you both know in your hearts that it's over, it would be wise for both of you to be mature, make arrangements, and move on for the sake of the kids.

What good is it to stay for the kids if all they see is unhealthy behavior from their mom and dad? It's just not fair to them. It's important to know this: When children witness this kind of behavior regularly, they can easily become scared, confused, angry, and feel isolated.

Bringing kids up in an environment that's unhealthy can also cause them to be mentally unstable. If your kids are old enough to understand, it can affect how they act in school and the relationships that they build with others.

I know that walking away from a relationship when you have kids can be a very difficult choice to make, but think about the kids. They don't deserve this. If they can't have their mom and dad behave like loving adults as it should be, then what good is staying? You're main goal should be raising happy, healthy, and good natured children. Living in a negative environment will soon rub off on them. Kids can feel when something's not right. Kids know how to get attention whether it is in a negative or positive way. They'll act out in ways that aren't normal because they're seeking attention. They'll start getting into trouble or hurting themselves simply because they don't quite understand what's going on. Most kids will begin to think that they're at fault.

You say that you're staying for the kids, but ask yourself, is it truly worth it? Seriously think it through.

I Made It

Although you tried to stop me...I made it. Although you didn't believe in me...I made it. Although you didn't support me...I made it. Although you left me all by myself...I made it. Although you wished me bad luck...I made it. Although you talked about me...I made it. Although I wanted to give up sometimes...I made it. Although you told lies about me...I made it. Although you took everything from me...I still made it. Although I didn't have a place to live at times...Lord I thank you, I still made it. Although I was hungry at times...I made it. Although I was sick in my body at times, by his grace and mercy, I made it through. Although I needed encouragement when I was feeling down and you turned your back on me, look at me now, I made it. Although I didn't have your blessings, apparently I had God's blessings because I made it...I'm making it...I'm living a good life now!

You made it! Don't allow what others didn't do for you stay in your heart. Focus on what's important. You made it through! That's all that matters. Don't waste your time holding on to resentments. Let them go. You made it! YOU made it!

Got LOVE

To be loved and to feel loved is such a blessing. Why would anybody want to take advantage of something so powerful?

Love is something that many people live their lives searching for, yearning for, and desperately wanting to feel. When people truly love you, they'll sometimes go out of their way for you just to see you happy. Love is kind, patient, understanding, and sacrificing. Love feels good, but can sometimes include long suffering. Real love is being able to be yourself around that certain person, when they don't judge you, and you can trust them. Love is being there when others turn their back. Love will cause you to stand up for a person when you know that they're right.

Some people will argue that love is complicated, but I beg to differ. We as humans make things complicated. When we love somebody, we will feel their pain when they're going through something and we will not let them go through it alone. Love is being strong when the other person is weak.

If you have supportive people in your life, don't take that for granted. Love is truly powerful and we should cherish it. Love sometimes means that you have to go the extra mile. Love means not giving up in the hardest of times. Real love isn't based on what you have

or what you can give. Real love comes deep from your
heart and soul. Got LOVE?

Be Careful who You associate With

We have to be very mindful of those whom we choose to associate with. You have to make smart decisions because we can't hang out with everybody. We have to pick and choose wisely who we allow into our space. Everybody you come into contact with cannot be considered a friend.

People sometimes come into our lives for a season to teach us something. Some people come into our lives to remind us of the type of people that we don't want to be associated with. Be careful who you call your friends. Be aware that some people have hidden agendas. Pay attention to their actions and to the things that they say and do. What I've found out is that a lot of people will jokingly say things that they actually mean. Trust me, it will eventually come out if you're around each other long enough.

You have to learn who you can put your trust in. Everybody can't keep your personal business to themselves. You can't hang out where everybody else hangs out. Be careful when you put your drink down and walk away. Be careful who you allow into your home. Be careful who you lend money to. Be careful who you hang out with. Some people have trouble written all over them. Be careful who you get into a car with. Be careful who you call your friends. Some people don't mean you any good. Trust me on that one! Be careful, very careful! Some people will only bring you down. I want to also point out that these people can be family too. All company is not good company. Evaluate the company that you keep. What does the company that you keep say about you? This is some good food-for-thought. A lot of people get caught up because they don't choose wisely. Be careful of who you associate with. It can end up costing you everything.

Just Because

I don't know about you, but I love being surprised with gifts "JUST BECAUSE."

On our birthdays, we may not want to admit it but, for the most part, we expect to get goodies. It's our birthday and that's what most people look forward to. We normally celebrate with family and friends and we look forward to opening and seeing what special gifts we've gotten this year.

We never know when it's our time to leave this earth. That's why I'm getting ready to make a valuable point and persuade you to do things differently if you don't already do so.

It doesn't have to be a "special day" for us to be kind to somebody. I'll hear a lot of people say: "I'll wait to buy that for him/her on their birthday." Why can't you just do it now? Why wait? It's not promised that we're going to make it to the next day. It's important that we make people feel special while they're still here. It amazes me how many people buy flowers when people pass away, and yet when they were alive, that thought didn't even cross their mind. If you feel it in your heart to do it, just do it. Take them on that special trip that they've been dreaming about. Take them out to their favorite restaurant. Attend the Ballet that they've been hinting at for the longest time. Take advantage of the now. Later is not promised. I also hear a lot of people say things like: "I wish...I should have...but it's too late. They're gone now."

When you do things for a person "just because," it makes them feel even more special because it's not, per say, a "special day." The fact that you thought of them and wanted to do something special for them gives them a feeling like no other. It's not the fact that you bought them a gift. It's the fact that you made that person feel appreciated. Who doesn't like to feel appreciated? Love and show people that you care about them while you can. Love with no regrets.

Love is not in Material Things

Love is very powerful! But many people relate love to gifts and what a person can do for them. We'll often times determine how much a person loves and cares for us based off of what they buy or give us. Love goes way deeper than that.

Real love feels good. When a person truly loves and cares for you, they have your best interest at heart. People who care for you show compassion for you, they listen to you, they respect you, they value the relationship that you share, they're attentive to your needs, and you won't have to question their love for you because it's in their actions. Love feels good, it doesn't hurt. Not to say that we don't make mistakes and hurt people unknowingly, but the key is that if you do something to hurt somebody that you love, you make it right by apologizing and making sure not to do it again.

Love understands, love is kind, love is spending quality time. Love can be felt in your touch and your acts of service. I would like to go a little deeper on acts of service. This is an area where you can really show how much you love and care for an individual, AND, it doesn't cost you anything but your time. You can wash their car, cook for them, give them a massage, write a poem or letter expressing how you feel for them, go on a long walk, go bike riding, have a picnic in the park, play board

103

games together, listen to some of your favorite music together, watch movies at home and enjoy some snacks.

I just gave you some great ideas, but you can think of some of the things that you personally enjoy doing on your own. The point is, to show love, you don't need money. You can't buy love. No matter how much money somebody spends on you, if there are any ill intentions behind what they're doing, it is invalid. You don't have to force real love. Remember that and keep it in your spirit.

My People, Let Kids Be Kids

I get so puzzled when I see some parents pushing their kids to grow up too fast.

You dress your little girls like they're grown women. You allow them to wear makeup way before their time. They know the lyrics to songs that they don't have any business listening to, and yet they don't know their ABC's, they can't count, they don't know their colors, shapes, or anything that is important for them to enhance their future.

You put weaves and hair pieces in their hair. REALLY! Take the time to take care of their hair so that it will properly grow. You allow them to watch whatever they want to on TV. They don't have a bedtime. They go to sleep whenever they want to. You show them how to do the latest dances as if they're grown women, dropping it low and popping their butts. And for the little boys, you get their ears pierced when they're young. How do you know that they want their ears pierced? They're little boys. Let them make that choice when they're old enough to do so. You teach them how to sag their pants. You try to toughen them up by play fighting with them and being rough with them. I've even witnessed and heard some of you teach your little ones how to say bad words and you actually think that it's funny.

Why can't you let your kids be kids? Allow them to enjoy their childhood free from ignorance. When I hear women refer to their little girls as "divas," all I can do is shake my head. They aren't divas. They're kids. Don't attach that name to them. Do you know what the definition of a diva is? It is not related to a little girl.

I get sickened when I hear parents refer to their son as "my lil' Nigga." What are you doing people? That's not what we're supposed to be teaching our kids. Give them a chance at something better. Give them tools that will help them be successful in life. Teach them how to speak properly and stop teaching them slang. Spend time with your little ones and teach them things that matter, not ignorant stuff. Stop corrupting their little souls with garbage.

I know that some of you are angered by this passage and you may even want to stop reading. Some of my passages are meant to convict you and bring awareness to you. If you're upset, then take a good look at yourself and at what you're doing. God blessed you with a child so that you could mold and shape them into good people. If you're busy teaching your child ignorant things, don't complain when your child gets older and starts disrespecting you and you have no control over them because their behavior is out of hand.

Remember: As a parent, you can choose to plant good or bad seeds within your child. It's up to us as parents to be good influences to our kids and to be good role models. There's nothing funny about a child cussing. There's nothing funny about a child throwing up gang signs. There's nothing funny about a child acting too grown up. There's nothing funny about a child being disrespectful. There's nothing funny about a child that loves to fight other kids.

Pay attention parents. You have a responsibility to do what's right. Do your job as a parent and raise your children to have respect for themselves and others. Raise them to have good morals and values.

Note: If this passage doesn't apply to you, then don't take offense. This is simply for the parents who do this. This passage is a wakeup call for certain people to look at themselves and do better.

No Longer

No longer will I allow you to talk down to me. No longer will I be afraid to speak and take up for myself. No longer will I allow your words to hurt me. No longer will I compare myself to the next person. No longer will I feel guilty for saying "NO." No longer will I be afraid to eat and enjoy the foods that I like. No longer will I give up on my goals. No longer will I start something and not finish it. No longer will I play second when I should be first. No longer will I allow you to physically or emotionally hurt me. No longer will I allow my precious time to be wasted on senseless things.

No longer will I be too busy to enjoy and create lasting memories with the people that I say I love. No longer will I be too busy to hear you. No longer will I take your kindness for weakness. No longer will I look for a way out. I will face my fears and disappointments. No longer will I make excuses. No longer will I put off today what is not promised to me tomorrow. No longer will I listen and accept your negativity. No longer will I carry the weight other peoples' problems. No longer will I be afraid to go out by myself. No longer will I allow my attitude to get the best of me. No longer will I be afraid to make important decisions for myself. No longer will I fail to follow through on what I said that I'd do. No longer will I doubt my abilities. I will give myself a chance. No longer will I allow my past to define who I should be. No longer will I be afraid to take chances.

Today I choose to live life more abundantly. I won't allow anything or anyone to get in the way of me having complete peace in my life. There's nothing like having inner peace.

Choose this day to make that change. Make the necessary adjustments in your life so that you can experience and live in complete peace too.

The Old Me Versus the New Me

The old me told me that I would never make it...but the new me says that I will make it. The old me told me that I was ugly and unattractive...but the new me tells me that I'm beautiful. The old me told me that I was a failure...but the new me says that I'm a winner, and that I can do anything that I put my mind to. The old me didn't believe in myself...but the new me says that I'm talented, gifted and that I'm somebody special. The old me was insecure about how I looked...but the new me has accepted me for who I am.

The old me was always being negative...but the new me has learned to be positive and speak good things into my life. The old me was mean and didn't know how to be a friend...but the new me has a lot of friends, and I value and appreciate them. The old me would speak without thinking...the new me has learned to respect other's feelings and to be respectful and use tact. The old me didn't care about life...but the new me understands that each day that I wake up; it's a gift from above.

The old me used to love to fight...but the new me understands that I don't have a right to put my hands on anybody, and that fighting is not okay nor attractive in any way, shape, or form. The old me used to lie...but the new me understands that lying on people will get them into a lot of trouble. The old me used to love to gamble...but the new me understands that I can spend my money on something much more valuable and important. The old me was shy and reserved...the new me is very outgoing and fun to be around. The old me was a follower...but the new me leads with confidence. The old me used to cuss everyday...the new me respects myself and shows class.

The old me used to get a joy out of bullying...the new me shows compassion for other people, and does whatever I can to help. The old me used to love to get high and drunk...but the new me appreciates my body and takes good care of it. The old me used to allow people to mistreat me...but the new me stands up for myself and demands nothing but respect.

This passage isn't personally about me. I simply wanted to give you a look at how someone can change if they wanted to. The choice is yours. What area of your life can you change to make yourself a better person? Did I mention anything in this passage that has prompted you to make a positive change in your life? Change is good. Look at the examples that I gave above. Doesn't the "new me" sound way better than the "old me?" Yes it does. Make your personal changes today.

Things are bad, now You want to Leave

My heart is hurting and it's hard to believe that, because we're going through hard times, you want to leave me. I thought that we were a team and that nothing could tear us apart. How could you even consider leaving me when I've done nothing but love and support you, and give you everything that you've ever desired?

Is it because our money is low and I can no longer afford to do the things that you're used to? I thought that we were better than that. I thought that our love was truly the real thing. Genuine and solid as a rock. I would never do anything to hurt you and I surely wouldn't tear you down when things are going badly. We've always lifted each other up and stood right by each other's side.

Where is the person that I knew before? I want the person back that always believed in me and always saw the best in me. I want the person back that vowed to stay around in the good and the bad times. I never realized that our love was based on what I could do for you. This aching in my heart just won't go away. I'm losing my best friend right in front of my eyes. When you look at me, the love is no longer there. And if I dare try to touch you, you just push my hands away and stare. Oh baby, why? Why are you doing this to me? I thought that our love would stand against any storm that we would face. I guess I have to accept that you're leaving me.

I've learned in my life that you can't make anyone stay that doesn't want to be there. I hope that you find happiness, my love, but remember these very words: "Love is not about money. Every relationship will have challenging times, but that's when you should stick together and don't give up on one another. But, if you want to go, I can't make you stay. I love you more than you'll ever know. It's just too bad you can't see that."

The Child You Never Had

I haven't forgotten about you although a lot of time has passed by. How could I? You were my first.

I often times wonder what you would have looked like. Would you have had my smile? Would you have had your dad's eyes? I bet anything that you would have had an outgoing personality just like me. I just know it! I know that you would have loved sports. Between the talent that your dad and I had, you would've been extremely talented too. You never forget your first. We both love you so much although we never got a chance to lay eyes on you. You will always live in our hearts.

I used to cry a lot, but over the years, I've gotten stronger. You would have been in your early twenties now. I want you to know that, at that particular time, I felt like I had no other choice. I was only a teenager and I was very confused. I know that I had no business having sex at 16. I had very low self-esteem and I was only trying to feel loved and get attention. But, now that I'm older, I realize that I was trying to get it in the wrong way. I felt lost and I was trying to find myself. On one hand, I knew that I had made a big mistake. I should've protected myself and had safe sex, but I didn't. On the other hand, as you started to grow inside of my stomach, I thought to myself: "This isn't right." I was just a kid myself. I couldn't have a baby. I made the difficult choice to abort you at 3 months, but in the back of my mind, I never stopped loving or thinking about you. I always wonder to this very day that, if I had kept you, what my life would be like. You could've been somebody great, but I'll never know because I chose to abort you so very long ago. I felt so guilty, but I asked God to please forgive me. I know that he has.

I wrote this passage for young girls, teenagers, and women. Make sure that you protect yourself if you're going to have sex. There's so much birth control available and there are many choices to choose from. If you know that you're too young, or you know that you're not ready to have a child, please protect yourself. No excuses! EVERYBODY makes mistakes, but making the same mistake over and over again is not acceptable. Just because you can get an abortion, doesn't mean you have the right to keep being irresponsible. Aborting a child is wrong! Don't get me wrong. If you've been violated, then that's different. You didn't ask for that. I'm talking about the people that don't take the necessary precautions and then end up pregnant, and then they want to get rid of the baby "just because."

The Lost Teenager

Being a teenager can be very difficult. Teenagers deal with peer pressure from every direction. They have the pressures of having sex, using drugs, drinking alcohol, bullying, trying to fit in with others, how to dress, and the list goes on and on.

Can you imagine dealing with all of this and NOT having a family that's supportive? Many teens feel alone and, unfortunately, they go through the most difficult times of their lives by themselves.

Everybody doesn't come from a home that is full of love. Some people grow up in homes and families that are nothing but dysfunctional. Imagine growing up in a home where you had nobody to talk to.

Your mom has never shown any interest in you and, everything positive that you try to do, she shoots it down with her negative words. Imagine never feeling loved by the one that gave birth to you. You never felt like you could be open, honest, or just be yourself around her. She didn't teach you how to love yourself. She didn't teach you how to respect yourself. She didn't ever say things that would help build your self-esteem. She never told you that she loved you. She never hugged you.

Let's talk about your father. Although you lived under the same roof, he was always drinking and angry. He certainly wasn't a man that you could look up to.

Whenever he spoke, he scared everybody in the house. He was a nice guy when he wasn't drinking, but those times were rare. He always looked so lost. You could see it in his eyes. You believe to this very day that he never wanted kids. You weren't allowed to call him dad.

I'll ask you again. Can you imagine what this is like? Have you lived this life or something similar? I'm referring to the lost teenager. Growing up and surviving with no love. IMAGINE it just for one minute.

For the teenagers going through this, I know it's rough, but keep your head up and know that you are somebody special! Many teens are being raised by hurt adults. It's a fact, when all you know it hurt, negativity, and pain, that's all you know how to give. Don't be angry with your parents because, for the most part, they don't know any better. You have to understand this: It's not normal for parents to mistreat their children. If they do, then something's very wrong with them and you have to understand that it most likely has nothing to do with you. It goes deeper than that. Hurt people hurt other people. That's why I write so much about learning how to love yourself even when nobody else does. I know it's very, very, very difficult to not have a parent's love, but somehow you have to be strong and love yourself.

There are a lot of people who grow up without their parents' love and still do well in life. That's because they gave themselves a chance. They didn't allow the lack of love to break them down. You have to know that YOU matter! Your parents are the ones that have a problem, not you. I know that it's hurtful, but don't let it break you down. Don't allow it to mess up your future. Don't allow somebody else's problems to become yours. You weren't asked to be born, but now that you're here, leave a great mark on this world and LIVE!

Be Careful what You Wish For

Have you ever wished that you were somebody else? Let me ask that question in a different way: Have you ever wished that you were in somebody else's shoes? I'm sure that we've all felt that way before. But, I've learned over the years that wishing that you were in somebody else's shoes is not a wise thought.

It seems pretty innocent when we're speaking. We say things like: "I wish I lived in a neighborhood like that. I wish I could afford to drive that kind of car. I wish that I could dress in expensive clothes all of the time. I wish that I could travel like them. I wish that I could dine out all of the time and not have to cook. I wish that I could send my kids to private school. I wish that I could be a stay-at-home mom. I wish that I didn't have to work and could still be able to live life nicely. I wish that I had money to spend on whatever I wanted to.

I wish that I could pick up and leave whenever I wanted to. I wish that I could afford to take a luxury vacation every year. I wish that I could wear the jewelry that he/she wears. I wish that I could afford everything new that comes out. I wish that I could afford to get pampered whenever I wanted to. I wish that I could own property in different parts of the world. I wish that I could save money, pay my bills, and vacation without worrying about money." I wanted to break it down so that you could have an up close look at the words that come out of our mouths sometimes.

Here's the danger in saying things like this: We don't know peoples' stories. Anyone can appear to be perfect on the outside, but you don't know what they're going through to have all of the things that you wish you had or could do. Some people have all of the things in the world and they can afford to go anywhere BUT, they are empty on the inside. Imagine that!

That's because THINGS can't complete you or make you feel whole. Things only make us feel good temporarily. When you find yourself thinking like this again, remember that you don't know what goes on behind closed doors. You don't know what people go through to keep what they have. Some people have it all, but they are still unhappy, stressed, depressed, and feel lonely on the inside. Some people live in big houses and don't even speak to one another. Be careful whose shoes you wish you were in. You could be wishing for pure hell.

Lack of Money

How many people do you know that miss out on things, special things in life due to a lack of money?

They miss out on their own prom because their parents don't have the money. They have to hold on tight to the limited funds that they have. The thought of buying a yearbook is out of the question because in their parents' eyes, that money can be used to buy food. Or what about the field trips that everybody's going on? They have to stay home and play sick because their parents can't afford to pay the extra money. They always make up reasons for why they can't hang out with their friends. Their friends are always out and about having fun and going different places but, because they don't have the funds, they opt not to go. They don't want their friends to know that their family is struggling and barely getting by.

Summertime is here and the sun is shining bright. But they are stuck being cooped-up in the house because their parents have to work extra long hours and they have to watch their siblings. They try their hardest not to be angry because, if their parents didn't work, they wouldn't have anything to eat or have a roof over their head.

But still, it just isn't fair. Why don't they get a chance to have fun like the others? Summer has passed and they have nothing exciting to share. Listening to all of their friends talk about all of the fun that they had and places that they went. All that they can do is fantasize and wish that they could have been there. Lack of money has robbed them of the simple things. They can't afford to eat out at the places that their friends eat. They carry their lunch bag with the same old things to eat. They dread a new school year because they don't know what it's like to wear new clothes. Their parents try their hardest to make ends-meet, but it never seems to be enough.

While their friends show off their new gifts, they sit and think to themselves "They're so lucky, they have it good!" They're not jealous of you because you're their friend. But still the question remains for them: "Why couldn't that be me, why was I the unlucky one?"

Lack of money robbed them. Lack of money hasn't been kind to them. Lack of money caused them to miss out on many things. Lack of money caused them pain. Lack of money caused them shame. Lack of money made them feel secluded. Lack of money made their childhood no fun at all.

I wrote this passage to show people just how blessed you are if you've never lived like this. Be thankful for what you've got. There are many people who wish that they could afford to do SOME things. So, the next time that you find yourself complaining about ANYTHING, remind yourself that this could be you or, if you're willing to be honest with yourself, this used to be you. You should stay mindful and be grateful in ALL things. It's so easy to complain about what you don't have, but what about the people who have nothing? They would give anything to have a little of what you have. Have a grateful and thankful heart!

Listen

If you really listen to people, you'll find out a lot about them. Pay attention to the types of things that they enjoy talking about. Do they talk about negative stuff all of the time and bring down your mood, or are they positive and a joy to be around? Are they always gossiping and telling you about other people's business? If so, be reassured that they're telling your business to somebody else too. Don't be fooled into thinking that you're special and that they wouldn't ever do that to you.

Do they talk about things that they're going to do, but never follow through? Are they always asking to borrow money but, on the flip side, they're always talking about how much they already have? They try to make you believe that they're happy in their relationship, but you can clearly see that there's no commitment whatsoever. They brag about how close their family is but, whenever you're around their family, they're always arguing and you can feel the tension in the room. He/She is always saying how much confidence they have, but you know that they suffer from insecurities because they're always complaining about everything.

Listening to people will definitely show you what they're really about. Try listening closely the next time that you're having a conversation. You'll start to catch people in lies and everything. Just listen. What do you hear?

This passage isn't meant to be negative. It's a wakeup call. You can't believe everything that you hear. But, if you learn to listen carefully, you'll decrease your chances of falling for blatant lies. As the saying goes "Some people talk loud, but aren't saying anything." They are only speaking empty words.

His Grace and Mercy

You may be feeling discouraged and down, but I encourage you to think about your life for a minute.

Have you ever asked yourself how you made it through your horrible relationship? Have you ever wondered how that bullet missed you? Have you ever questioned why you didn't lose your mind after all of the stuff that you've been through in your life? Have you ever wondered how you managed to stay out of trouble and not get caught up with going in and out of prison when your family has a history of getting into trouble with the law? Have you ever asked yourself how you got that job and you know that you weren't qualified to do it? Have you ever questioned how it's possible that you grew up in a family where drugs and alcohol is an addiction to many, and somehow it skipped over you?

Have you ever questioned why you were the only one in your family to finish high school and the first to go to college? Have you ever questioned how you survived that horrible car accident? Have you ever questioned why you don't have a serious health condition when everybody in your family has serious health issues? Have you ever wondered why you show so much love, but your family is dysfunctional and THEY never show love? Do you wonder why you're so successful, when everybody else in your family struggles just to get by? Do you ever wonder why you're so good at handling money, when everybody else can't save money to save their life? Do you ever question how you remain focused and get the job done when most people that you know are easily distracted by other things that are going on? Do you ever question how you are so responsible when others don't care about being irresponsible?

I'll tell you what it is. It's God's GRACE and MERCY!

I Will not Give up on Me

I will not give up on me. For I have been down that road before. I remember what it's like to walk away from something that I was so passionate about. I remember what it's like to walk away from my dreams. I know what it feels like to settle for less than what I deserve. I know what it feels like to pretend that everything is okay when on the inside I'm hurting and full of pain. I know what it feels like to have sleepless nights...tossing and turning, wondering if things will ever change.

I know what it feels like to be waiting by the phone, hoping that you'll call. I know what it feels like when you love somebody and they don't love you back. I know what it feels like to give your heart to someone over, and over, and over again. I know what it feels like to be lied to...it didn't seem to faze you one bit. I know what it feels like to not be put first in someone's life because drugs and alcohol have the first priority. I know what it feels like to have low self-esteem. I KNOW...I KNOW! I know what it's like to have a child and you think that it's going to be the changing factor in your relationship. I know what it feels like to love someone so much, and yet they still don't get it.

I know what it's like to give up on me. I now know just how important I am. I count, and I deserve the VERY best!

128

I am special...I am loving...I am loyal...I am beautiful on the inside...I am strong, and I am worthy and deserving of genuine love. I know my self-worth, so I will not give up on me! I will not give up on me! I will NOT give up on me! I am NOT a victim, I am victorious. Amen!

I want my readers to see themselves in this passage. Keep telling yourself that you won't give up on YOU. Keep saying it until you believe it. Keep saying it until you achieve it. Do NOT give up on you. You're much too important. Believe that!

Please Don't Text and Drive

Some people just don't get it! I don't think that they truly realize the dangers of texting and driving. Please understand this: TEXTING AND DRIVING JUST DON'T MIX. I can't seem to wrap my mind around how someone can think that they can text while they drive and still pay attention to the road. If you look at it, it clearly doesn't make any sense.

I challenge you to look at it this way: How would you feel if you killed somebody because you were texting? Really think about it. How could you live with yourself knowing that you chose to text and not pay attention rather than be a responsible driver while on the road? Remember, I didn't say to think about if you hurt someone. I said if you KILLED someone.

Let's take it a little deeper and bring it closer to home. How would you feel if you received a phone call telling you that one of your loved-ones, close friends, or somebody that you associated with was killed by somebody who was texting and driving? I'm pretty sure that you'd be outraged and you wouldn't have any understanding of why that happened.

You are putting people's lives at risk when you selfishly take it upon yourself to text while you drive. I can only imagine how families feel when they get a call that they've lost someone because of somebody else's irresponsibility. WAKE UP PEOPLE! You are not thinking rationally when you choose to do this. If you receive a text and you feel that it is important, PULL OVER and check it. Nine times out of ten, the text is NOT important anyways. Advise your family and friends that if they need to contact you immediately, they should call back-to-back instead of texting you so that you know to pull over and take that important phone call. You have a responsibility to drive safely.

What about the days when we didn't have cell phones? What did you do then? Think about it. Please understand that looking at and answering a text isn't worth hurting or killing yourself or somebody else. It's just not worth it! Make a vow today that you won't text and drive. Do your part to help keep the roads safe!

*Imagine this. What if you're a parent and you were on your way to pick up your child from school and, suddenly, right in front of your face, your child is struck by a driver. You hop out of the car and immediately run to see what happened. The other driver jumps out their vehicle saying how sorry they are. You asked how they couldn't have seen your child, and they admit that they were texting and driving. Your child was lucky this time, they didn't lose their life, but they will NEVER be able to walk again.

*What about if your grandparent(s) was crossing in the cross walk like they were supposed to be doing and, because the driver wasn't paying attention, they ran the stop sign. Luck was not on their side. They were killed instantly. The impact was too much for their bodies to handle.

*Let's say that your spouse or your girlfriend/boyfriend called and told you that they were on their way home. On their way home, they stopped at your favorite store to surprise you with a special gift. As they were making a turn into the parking lot of your favorite store, a teenager that just got their license wasn't paying attention because they were busy fighting via text with their mate and BOOM, they killed your loved-one on impact.

I hope that you see what texting and driving can do. It's not worth it. PLEASE get this in your spirit. PLEASE!!!

Who Says that Men Can't be Sensitive

I personally find it attractive when a man can show his sensitive side. But, society puts a lot of pressure on men to be a "MANS MAN."

Why is it looked upon as being weak if a man cries? Excuse me, the last time that I checked, men have emotions and feelings too. Why is it that when a man does his own laundry, cooks, and cleans he must have a little "sugar in his tank?" Meaning it's a possibility that he could be gay. This is just plain nonsense! How about if a man likes to keep himself up and get manicures and pedicures? No, not all men find this to be masculine, but what's wrong with a man wanting to keep his hands and feet descent? How many women can honestly say that they like men with nasty looking finger nails and rough, disgusting looking feet?

I think that it's safe to say ZERO! Some women think that if a man is too clean-cut, then he must be gay. Do you really believe that? As I reflect back to the 50's and 60's to be exact, men were ALL neat and well put together. But, for some reason in today's society, we don't give our men a chance. We can sometimes be too judgmental. What about if a man wears his pants to fit nicely? Some may think that if he's not sagging, then he's a "square" or something else.

Really take a look at the examples I've given. Women: We need to get it together. There's nothing wrong with a man wanting to be nicely groomed and wanting to look good. If your man needs to cry, let him cry. Don't make him feel bad because he needs to let out his emotions. That's a good thing! We need to learn how to build up our men instead of tearing them down. Now that's Real Talk!

Let there be LIGHT

Let there be light in how you treat others. Let there be light in your attitude. Let there be light in your personality. Let there be light in your behavior. Let there be light in your conversations. Let there be light in your thinking. Let there be light in how you carry yourself.

When people come into contact with you, does your light shine? Take a minute to think about it. Are you one of those people that like to start arguments? Are you one of those people that bring down the mood? Are you one of those people who gossip all of the time? Are you one of those people that are always negative and have nothing positive to say? Are you one of those people that others dislike to see coming? Are you one of those people that are self-centered? Are you one of those people that like to start rumors and keep up drama? Are you one of those people that have a bad attitude?

What kind of person are you? That's a valid question that most people don't take the time out to think about. If your light isn't shining or it's dull, it's time to make some changes in your life. NOBODY likes to be around people who bring them down. BUT, there's no need to feel bad if you do some of the things that I've pointed out. This is an eye-opener for you and an opportunity for you to make some changes. Change is good, especially if it's going to better you as a person. I challenge you to really take a look at YOU. What do you see?

Loneliness

Beware of loneliness. It'll surely cause you to do things that you'll later regret.

Loneliness will have you doing things that you never thought you'd do. Loneliness will have you hanging out in places where you know you don't belong. Loneliness will cause your mind to think about things that are way out of your character. Loneliness will have you lying, cheating, sneaking around, making excuses about the things that you're doing, and have you start to believe that it's okay. Loneliness will have you fantasizing about things that you wouldn't normally dare act upon. Loneliness will eventually cause you to question: "What's wrong with me, why hasn't anybody chosen me?" It will slowly tear down your self-esteem. Loneliness will cause you to hang out with the wrong crowd. Loneliness can attach itself to you and, before you know it, you'll become a slave to whatever it wants you to do.

I'll say it again. Beware of loneliness! Loneliness can break you ALL the way down. It can have you addicted to sex, drugs, alcohol, hurting yourself, and so many other things that are unhealthy to your well-being.

That is why it's so important to love yourself. Things and people cannot complete you or make you whole. You have to reach deep down in your soul and tell yourself: "I may be lonely, but I will NOT subject my soul

to hell. I will not lower myself for a quick fix in my life."
You have to understand, it's just that...A quick fix. Take
the time and play the tape all the way through. Ask
yourself: "If I do this or if I do that," what will be the
consequences? How will this affect my life? Then go a
little further. Ask yourself the big question: "Is this worth
ruining my life?"

We have to value our lives. Each day that we wake
up and breathe, it is a gift that shouldn't be taken for
granted. It's important to know that everything has its
place and time. Learn to be strong and content by
yourself. Your time will come. But, in the meantime, love
yourself. Take the time to get to know who you really are
as a person. Be patient and remember this: When we try
to rush and make things happen before its time, it's sure
to fail. Take this precious time to work on yourself, get to
know yourself better, and don't forget to love yourself.
Self-Love is important and needed. You are important!
You matter! You count!

Why do You Treat Me so Bad

I love you with all of my heart and soul, and yet you get pleasure out of treating me so badly. I respect you in every way possible. I stand beside you and support you because I care for you dearly. I've never once disrespected you, but you find it so easy to disrespect me. I do special things to show you how much I care, but I don't seem to matter to you. I try to hug and kiss you, but all you do is push me away, saying how tired you are or that you have other things to do. I cook special meals for you and I don't even get a thank you. I go to work every day and save money for us. You'd rather take your money and spend it elsewhere. I never get to see it.

     I buy you cards expressing my love for you. I've never even received ONE from you. I massage your back and feet when I see that you've had a very long day, but when you see that I'm tired, you just look away. There have been times when I've had tears in my eyes, but you never show any concern or ask me what's wrong.

     After all that I've done for you, why do you like to treat me so badly? I don't understand how you can't see my hurt and pain. When I get dressed up and I'm looking my best, I never get compliments from you, but I'm always quick to say kind words to you. I don't understand why you treat me this way. I just don't understand.

I have given you a very powerful example of what some people go through in their relationships. I need you to really search yourself on this one. You shouldn't be asking yourself: "Why do they treat me so badly?" You should be asking yourself: "Why am I allowing someone to treat me like this?" Why do I stay and subject myself to this kind of pain? Why do I settle for this treatment? Why do I make excuses for their behavior? Only you know the answer to these questions.

Search deep inside of yourself and figure out how and why you ended up in this kind of relationship. Nobody, and I mean NOBODY, deserves to be treated like this. You're the only one that can change the situation.

Remember, nobody can do things to us and get away with them unless we allow them to. You noticed that I said unless WE allow it. Get out of that bad situation. Don't make any excuses. Get out!

Put Yourself First

Some people may say that, when you put yourself first, you're being selfish. Putting yourself first doesn't mean that you're being selfish at all. It means that you care about yourself and that you understand that it's important to take good care of yourself. It also means that you love yourself enough to know that you are important. Let's take a walk down memory lane.

Have you ever compromised and said "Yes" just to please someone else, but it wasn't something that you really wanted to do? Have you ever given up on something that you were passionate about just so that your spouse would stop nagging? Have you ever stopped socializing or hanging out with your friends because your girlfriend or boyfriend didn't like them? Have you ever packed up and moved to another town/city/state because the other person thought that it would be best? Have you ever turned down a great opportunity because someone said "I've tried that before, what a waste of time?"

Have you ever had somebody ask you when you're having kids and you just respond by saying "OH, we're just waiting for the right time," when you know that your mate has already told you that he/she doesn't want any kids? Did you settle for a vehicle that you really didn't want, but somebody talked you into buying the one that they thought was better? Did you cut your hair because people were always saying it was "too long?" Did you kiss, have sex, or go too far before you were ready because you were scared that, if you didn't give in, it would run off somebody that you really liked?

There are so many scenarios like this that we face every day. If we would simply just slow down, take a step back, and evaluate what's taking place, we will see that we give in to certain situations way too easily. I'm sure by now that you will agree that putting yourself first is a good thing.

So, the next time that someone tells you "Stop being selfish," look them directly in the eyes with confidence and say "I can't afford NOT to be selfish. I love and care about myself."

No Explanation

I miss our long talks over the phone. Joking, laughing, and reminiscing about the good old days. I remember the fun that we used to have every summer when we used to go to the beach with our basket full of goodies, games, and our favorite drink, ice cold lemonade, freshly made by your mother. Oh, what fun we used to have spending the whole day together until the sun went down. Those were the days. I miss you dearly.

I remember how we used to take long walks along the Pier and tell each other our deepest secrets. We were truly inseparable. Everybody thought that we were sisters because of the love and closeness we both shared. I still remember your favorite flavor of ice cream, Rocky Road with hot fudge on top. Do you still enjoy drawing and painting? I always thought that you had a great talent. I wonder where you went. You left without saying a word. I'll never forget you. I pray for you all of the time.

I thought that what we shared was real. I thought that you loved me without any doubts. I truly loved you. I miss the way you used to hold me when we would be watching a movie and you knew that I was scared. Or what about our date nights on Thursdays? We both thought that we were chefs, always trying out new recipes that we found in our cookbook. We were never good at baking, so we would laugh at each other when things didn't turn out too well. I miss listening to music and pretending that we were on stage in front of millions of fans. Although it was just me and you, we both supported each other with a yell and shout, as if it was coming from real fans. I remember that you used to have terrible allergies in the spring time. I used to take good care of you, making sure you had the medicine that you needed. I don't understand what went wrong. You didn't say goodbye to me. I had to hear that you were leaving through a mutual friend. I will always love you.

I miss my best friend and I know you miss me too. I came home from school looking for you, but you were nowhere to be found. Your mom had a weird look on her face. I tried to approach her, but her look stopped me right where I was standing. I started to worry about you and I didn't know what to do. We were only in the 5th grade. As I walked around our neighborhood hoping that I'd see your face, instead I saw an ambulance taking you away. I later heard that you had passed away. I miss my friend and I know that you miss me too. But I know that you're in heaven watching over me. Why did you have to go this way? You were such a fun person and you had the most loving heart. I'll never know what happened, but I know that I will always keep you in my heart.

I have shared with you **4** different stories above. Have you ever had a friend or somebody close to you leave with no explanation? Words unspoken...words unspoken... words unspoken. There was no closure at all. Words unspoken...words unspoken...words unspoken.

I Commend You

I commend you because you don't allow your disability to hinder you. Although you are confined to a wheelchair, you always have a smile on your face. You are one of the happiest people that I have ever come into contact with. Your smile lightens up any room. Even though you can't walk, talk, or take care of yourself, there's something very special about you. I love you dearly Tomisha, my dearest cousin.

I commend those who have a disability and still live their lives and enjoy it to the fullest. I'm so thankful for the SPECIAL OLYMPICS for giving these people a chance to shine. When I see you all enjoying yourselves playing your favorite sport, I think to myself: "What a blessing." I also commend the parents that are involved in helping your lives be more fulfilled with sports. I commend you for your strength, dedication, love, and support for your special one.

I give special thanks to the people that commit and dedicate their time to people with special needs. It truly takes someone special to do your job. I salute you! For all of the parents that chose to take care of your child with a special-need and not put them away in a home or facility, God bless you! I know that it takes great strength to do what you do. And for those who felt like you had no other choice but to put your child in a facility or home because you felt like you couldn't handle it, don't feel bad. Just make sure that you check on them, visit them, and stay involved. Don't forget, you're still the parent and that shouldn't change your love.

I want to end the passage on this note: We are ALL so blessed to have our health and strength, and to be able to be in our right mind. Don't take that for granted! There are so many people in this world that don't have the same opportunities as you. Remember that, and be grateful on a daily basis.

I dedicate this passage to my cousin Tomisha and all of the other people that have a disability, or are somebody that's taking care of a person with a special-need. I pray that God continues to bless you with the strength to do what you do. Thank God for you!

Stop Allowing Time to Pass You By

As humans, we like to set goals for ourselves and sometimes we'll put a time frame on it. We'll say to ourselves: "I'm going back to school to finish my degree. I'm going to start working out. I'm going to start eating healthy. I'm going to walk a marathon. I'm going to open up my own business," and we tend to go on and on about what we are going to do and never get to the first thing that we set out to accomplish. We allow time to pass us by without even realizing it. The reason why is because we keep making excuses. Before you know it, days, months, and years have passed.

Stop allowing time to pass you by. It's time out for putting our goals on the back burner. When we speak about doing something that's important to us, we need to act on what we speak of with a sense of urgency.

I want you to take a look back over your life. How many opportunities have you allowed to pass you by? One is too many. We can change that by changing our attitudes. When you have a goal or a dream, you have to keep it alive.

Put your plans in motion and don't stop until you get there. Don't allow your goals, dreams, or passions in life to be things of the past because you allowed TIME to pass you by. Time it too precious to be wasted. Once time has passed, we can't get it back. You have to be mindful and do better.

Never Felt Love

I wrote this passage for my readers that have never felt love in their lives. As I wrote this passage, I touched on many areas in which a person can feel the pain of not feeling loved.

My heart goes out to the little boys and girls that grew up in the foster-care system. I'm talking about the kids that were placed in a home where the foster parents only cared about the money. My heart goes out to you and my heart aches to know that you were treated so badly and that horrible things happened to you. You were never loved, only mistreated. You were bounced around from home to home and there was never any stability. You weren't treated with love and you didn't feel safe. You were not protected nor were you taken care of. Although the foster parents are getting money for you, you never get anything new.

You live in an environment that is negative and full of hate. You're forced to clean up behind everybody else, and you feel like you're their personal maid. You don't do well in school because you don't have a positive or quiet place to study. It's always loud and people are always coming in and out of your house. You wonder to yourself: "Does the Social-Worker know about this?" But, of course, you never say anything because you know better. You know what pain feels like. That's all you've ever known. The reason why you're in foster-care is because your mom couldn't stay off drugs and you never knew who your father was. Your life was terrible from the start. Living with your mom wasn't any different from foster-care. You barely had anything to eat and you became accustomed to her beatings. She would leave you at home all by yourself. You've never had a fair chance. All you know is pain, suffering, and the feeling of being unloved.

Let's talk about the people that grew up in a so-called "good home." You had your parent(s), but you still felt unloved. You could never do anything to make your parent(s) proud of you. You lived in the same home, but you barely communicated. They weren't involved in anything that you did. Your family never sat down to eat together. You never received any hugs or kisses. Although your parent(s) had great careers, they had no idea of how to balance family and work. Their work got more attention than you did. They showered you with gifts, but what you really wanted was their love. You never enjoyed the family vacations because there was always a lot of tension. In public, everything seemed perfect, but you knew what things were like behind closed doors. Everybody wishes that they were in your shoes, but they don't have a clue of how empty you feel inside. You've never felt loved and you don't feel worthy.

151

What about the people that grew up with no family? You always found yourself sleeping where ever you could. You had a hard life and you knew nothing about love. The streets were all you knew. You learned how to hustle at an early age. Your heart is hardened and you find it difficult to trust anyone. Most of the people that you know do bad things just to get by. Your life has been hell ever since you can remember. You've never had a kind word spoken to you. You cause people pain because that's all you've ever known. There are many feelings that are pinned up inside of you. You hide the feelings that you have because you don't want to face the emotions that come with the fact that you don't have any family. You're alone and your life is very lonely and cold. You have envy and hate in your heart for others. You're angry on the inside, but you put a smile on your face like everything is okay. The truth is that you just want to feel loved. You want to feel wanted. You want somebody in your life that cares. You want love. You want family. You want to feel normal.

I wrote these passages just to prove a point: If you have received love in your life, don't take it for granted. As you see, there are many people from different walks of life that have never known what it's like to be loved.

Letting go is Hard When You Still Care

We've been an item for quite some time now, but I know that what I once felt for you is now gone. I've tried so hard to keep the love alive, but I have to be honest with myself, I'm not IN LOVE with you anymore. I love you and will always care for you, but I haven't been "in love" for a long time now. I don't know how I got here, but it's a fact that I have to face. I never thought that breaking up would be this difficult for me.

I guess that when you care for somebody this deeply, it makes all of the difference. This is very hard for me to deal with. I don't want to hurt you or cause you any pain. I know deep in my heart how much you truly love and care for me. You're such a good man and I don't understand why I'm feeling like this. There's nothing that you wouldn't do for me. I know that you love me like crazy and that most people envy what we have. So why am I feeling this way, WHY?

I've thought about cheating, but deep down inside that's not what I want to do. I just want to be free and I can't explain why. I wish that I had a valid explanation for you. You've done nothing wrong, it's all on me. I have this burning desire to live a little bit on the wild side. I feel like there's so much more that I need to see and experience in life. Am I crazy for feeling this way? Maybe, but I just can't shake this feeling that I have.

Oh God, please help me! I need you now. I know that I shouldn't be thinking this way. I could be making the biggest mistake of my life. Without a doubt, I know that you love and care for me, but something's changed. I've been trying to hold on to something that has run its course, but I think that it's time that I let go. I will always love you and I will always care about you, but we both deserve complete happiness.

I wrote this passage because I know that a lot of people deal with this exact problem in their relationships. It's better to be upfront and honest with one another. If you feel that the relationship is over, it's best to move on if you're completely sure and you don't feel anything in your heart for your mate anymore. It'll pay off in the end. A lot of people say that they stay because they don't want to hurt the person that they're involved with. But, if you stay in a relationship that you're not happy in, you'll eventually hurt them more than you know. It's okay to leave. Just leave on a good note. I know it's difficult because you care, but care enough to move on and not string them along giving them false hope.

My Hopes and Prayers for You

I pray that my book has impacted your life for the better. I pray that the topics that I've written about have enlightened you, encouraged you, convinced you to do better, given you food-for-thought, and brought awareness to you. The whole purpose of me writing this book was for the PEOPLE. Helping you uncover and see yourself for who you truly are. When we know better, we should strive to do better. I knew that when I started writing this book, I didn't want to hold back. I wanted to deliver it to you raw and uncut. I didn't want to sugar-coat anything. You can't grow as a person if you aren't willing to except the truth. My purpose was to push you to dig deep and uncover what's really inside of you.

I pray with all of my heart that the passages I've written about will help you move forward and become a better you. I pray that you will be blessed with good health, and that your life will be prosperous in every area of your life. Move forward doubting nothing, and allow the words that I wrote to stick with you. Allow them to minister to your heart. My prayer for you is to have complete peace and happiness within. I also pray that God will fill your minds and hearts with great wisdom, knowledge, and insight. Move forward and be blessed in everything you do.

God bless you and thank you for reading my book, *Overcoming Life's Obstacles*.

Special Note: If you enjoyed this book, and it has impacted you in any kind of way, please write a review on Amazon.com. I want to hear your stories. I want to know how my book has had an impact on your life. Thank you for your support!!!

36316421R00098

Made in the USA
San Bernardino, CA
19 July 2016